THE NEW MARXISM

ABOUT THE AUTHOR

RICHARD T. DE GEORGE, chairman of the department of philosophy at the University of Kansas, is the author of *Patterns of Soviet Thought* and *Classical and Contemporary Metaphysics*, co-author of *Science and Ideology in the Soviet Union* and the editor of *Ethics and Society*. A graduate of Fordham University, he holds M.A. and Ph.D. degrees in philosophy from Yale University and a Ph.B. from the University of Louvain. Mr. De George has been a lecturer in philosophy at Columbia University, a Fulbright Fellow, and the recipient of many academic honors. He has undertaken postdoctoral studies at the University of Fribourg and in the U.S.S.R., and is a frequent contributor to the leading scholarly journals.

THE NEW MARXISM

SOVIET AND EAST EUROPEAN MARXISM SINCE 1956

by Richard T. De George

PEGASUS  NEW YORK

Acknowledgment is made to the following sources for permission to use
material previously published:
Monthly Review Press: Adam Schaff, *A Philosophy of Man*. Copyright ©
1963 by Adam Schaff.
Iris Hibernia: Richard T. De George, "The Soviet Concept of Man," *Iris
Hibernia: Aspects of Communism*, 1964.
Inquiry: Richard T. De George, "Morality, Ethics, and East-European
Marxism," *Inquiry*, IX, No. 1, 1966.

Preface

■ Since Khrushchev's 1956 speech on Stalin, a great deal has happened in the Soviet Union and Eastern Europe. There has been a shift from Moscow as the center of the communist movement to what has become known as "polycentrism." The brute force associated with Stalin's reign has been mitigated, the countries of Eastern Europe have asserted their nationalism, and there has been a noticeable thaw in the cold war. Has there been any corresponding change in theory, in the Marxism or Marxism-Leninism which flourishes in the countries of Eastern Europe? This book is an attempt to answer this question by describing the changes which have taken place, the relation of present positions to previous ones, and the divergencies among the East European Marxists. It further attempts to evaluate the significance of these developments. Though my primary emphasis is on theory and especially on Marxist ideology and philosophy, other aspects necessarily enter into the discussion.

At the risk of oversimplification, we can roughly characterize the situation of Marxist theory in several of the countries in which we shall be primarily interested. In the Soviet Union, which represents the most dogmatic end of the spectrum, all the philosophers who are allowed to publish are officially Marxist-Leninists. Though the official position is that they all agree on the truth and truths of Marxism-Leninism, there are more differences among them than they are willing to admit. In Hungary also all the philosophers who are allowed to publish are Marxist-Leninists. They claim to disagree among themselves; but they disagree less than they claim to. In Poland philosophers are allowed to publish who are not Marxists or Marxist-Leninists, and among the Marxists there are significant disagreements. And in Yugoslavia, which represents the least dogmatic end of the spectrum,[1] though almost all of the philosophers claim to be Marxists, they differ with one another to such an extent that it is sometimes difficult to tell from their writings that they are Marxists at all.

Despite these differences, Marxist ideology remains one of the ties which bind Eastern Europe together. We find diversity amidst unity, and continuity amidst change. The new Marxism is not radically new. At the same time, especially in some of its East European variants, it is clearly different from the static, dogmatic Marxism-Leninism of the Soviet Union under Stalin.

The present work is based on a wide range of official and popular writings from the Soviet Union and Eastern Europe, both in the original and in translation, as well as on personal observations in these countries. The manuscript was written in large part during time made available to me by a grant from the University of Kansas. Chapters three and five of the present work are based upon articles of mine which appeared in *Iris Hibernia*[2] and *Inquiry*[3] respectively, and some of the material has been reused here with the permission of the editors.

R D G
December, 1967

---

[1] This book was completed before the liberalization which took place in Czechoslovakia during the early months of 1968. As it goes to press, the extent and permanency of the liberalization are not yet clear, and no new significant Marxist works have appeared.

[2] Richard T. De George, "The Soviet Concept of Man," *Iris Hibernia: Aspects of Communism*, 1964, pp. 14–28.

[3] Richard T. De George, "Morality, Ethics and East European Marxism," *Inquiry*, IV (1966), No. 1, pp. 11–29.

Contents

THE NEW MARXISM

Continuity, Accommodation, and Change in Marxist Doctrine

1

■ Karl Marx is at least nominally a towering figure of authority in all Marxist literature. Acknowledgment of his authority is perhaps the only common element in the great variety of Marxist positions. Yet for the most part today's Marxists are not primarily concerned with an historical analysis or interpretation of the works of Karl Marx. The work of reconstructing the thought of Marx in its various stages of development, of carefully and critically correlating what he says in one passage with what he says in another, of attempting an historically accurate presentation of the writings of Marx as a whole is the concern of a small group known as "Marxologists." They are scholars, historians of ideas, interested in the nineteenth-century theories of the German exile who lived most of his productive adult life in London, who was a leader of the labor movement, a co-author of the *Communist Manifesto,* the economist-author of *Capital,* a sometime philosopher, social theorist, and historian. Those whom I shall refer to as the "new Marxists" are thinkers of another breed.

The doctrines vaguely labeled "Marxism" are those contained in the writings of Karl Marx. But Marx's writings are not systematic. Marx himself, as an active thinker and leader, did not come to his theories all at once. They developed and changed as he encountered new situations, new ideas, new problems, and as his own interests shifted. He started out as a student of philosophy, and earned a doctoral degree in this field. He was strongly influenced by Hegelianism, with which he remained infected throughout his life. But he turned against Hegel's idealism in favor of what he called "materialism"—a vague term to cover a vague orientation. He became convinced that it is not ideas that change the world, and equally convinced that the world needed changing. Society can be changed, he thought, only by changing its economic and social conditions. He consequently shifted his major theoretical interest from philosophy to economics, a shift which resulted in his writing his magnum opus *Capital*, of which he was able to complete and publish only the first volume.

Yet Marx's writings are voluminous. They form a huge reservoir from which his followers have often made arbitrary selections. Varying interpretations of his work began even before his death, prompting his famous statement: "All I know is that I am not a Marxist."[1] In 1932 some of his early philosophical writings were published for the first time. They had been completely unknown to the Marxists of the nineteenth and early twentieth centuries and have supplied a source which is being tapped by some of the new Marxists.

The writings of Marx were explained, systematized, elaborated, and developed by Engels, who in the process added many of his own ideas. For Lenin and his followers, as well as for many others, "Marxism" came to refer to the contents of the works of both authors. These in their turn were commented upon in diverse ways, applied to changing circumstances, corrected, modified, and revised. The interpretations and additions of Lenin became dominant in the Soviet Union during the period following the October Revolution in Russia. During Stalin's reign the official Marxist theory in the Soviet Union became known as "Marxism-Leninism," a term still used today. Marxism-Leninism was promulgated and taught widely within the Soviet Union. The only orthodox interpretation of Marxism-Leninism during Stalin's rule in the Soviet Union was Stalin's, whose pronouncements on everything from linguistics to philosophy, from economics to biology were eulogized as milestones on mankind's path to truth.

In 1956 Khrushchev in his now famous speech denounced certain aspects of Stalin's rule. Stalin's stranglehold on theory was deprecated and some changes in both theory and practice were initiated. After Stalin's death, however, the primacy of the Soviet Union was questioned by the so-called satellite nations of Eastern Europe. Stalin's interpretations of Marxism-Leninism were challenged not only in the Soviet Union, but also in other countries of Eastern Europe, and the resulting reinterpretations sometimes differed. Communism in general had changed from a monocentric to a polycentric movement, with several hubs of influence, power, and interest. The official, quasi-official, and unofficial interpretations of Marxism have consequently proliferated.

By the "new Marxism" I mean those theories termed either "Marxist" or "Marxist-Leninist" by those expounding them in either the Soviet Union or the other countries of Eastern Europe. These are not the theories of Marxologists but the living thought of contemporaries who claim to be following in Marx's intellectual footsteps. The "new Marxism" refers therefore not to one specific present-day interpretation of Marxist doctrine, but to a family of such interpretations. I shall pay only passing attention to the Marxisms of Western Europe and America for, interesting though they may be, they are uninstitutionalized and generally have not been linked with political power, and thus do not play a prominent role in their respective societies.

The Soviet Union is still the leading socialist country which has officially adopted the Marxist-Leninist ideology. I shall therefore take the ideological developments there since Stalin's denunciation in 1956 as the central topic of discussion. But changes in Marxist theory in some of the other East European countries are more radical and more interesting, and I shall refer to these developments by way of contrast. From Eastern Europe we can see how Soviet theory may later evolve and we can become more acutely aware of the richness, ambiguity, and variety of the interpretations of which Marx's writings are susceptible.

Why Marx?

The new Marxism prides itself on its independence and originality. It contrasts itself with the Marxism and Marxism-Leninism of the Stalinist period in Marxist theory—roughly from 1930 through 1956. During this time the only interpretation of the writings of Marx, Engels, and Lenin which was allowed was that of Stalin. His brief statements in "Dialectical and Historical Materialism" which appeared in *The History of the Communist Party of the Soviet Union (Bolsheviks): Short Course* marked the limits of interpretation within which theoreticians worked. These few remarks were praised as creative and original interpretations of Marxist-Leninist doctrine and were expanded verbally, but not in content, into textbooks. These and the *Short Course* formed the pap on which many party workers and Soviet citizens were nurtured. In 1947 Stalin himself paved the way for more diversification and discussion within Marxist-Leninist theory, and in 1950 his letters to *Pravda* on Marxism and linguistics widened the road still further. But the limits of controversy and discussion were still set by the Communist Party of the Soviet Union and especially by its leaders. Soviet theoreticians mark the end of the Stalinist era as the beginning of their new freedom in theoretical matters. In fact, however, Soviet theoretical innovations are still quite meager. On the whole they represent continuations of changes instituted under Stalin and begun before his death.

After World War II Marxism-Leninism was brought into the satellite countries by the respective communist parties in power. Generally speaking, as in politics, so in theory, the satellites followed the lead of the Soviet Union.

According to the official spokesmen of the Eastern bloc a free wind swept the bloc with the denunciation of Stalin. The influence of the Soviet Union over the other East European countries was unquestionably diminished, though it still remains an important factor. The changes in Marxist theory which have taken place in Poland are wider than those in the USSR, and changes are noticeable in Hungary and Czechoslovakia also. But in all these countries the orthodox doctrine is still determined by the leaders of the respective communist parties. Even in Yugoslavia, where Marxist theory is the freest and most diversified in Eastern Europe, there are limits beyond which it is not permissible to go, as the case of Djilas and more recently that of Mihajlov have shown.

The much touted ideological freedom is considerable only in contrast with the strictness of the early and middle Stalinist periods. For the communist parties in each country are still the watchdogs of ideological purity, and the official ideology which is widely taught and disseminated is exclusively Marxist or Marxist-Leninist. To those raised and living in pluralistic societies the natural question is: Why Marx? Why do the philosophers and the social theorists, the historians and the ideologists all quote Marx or Marx, Engels, and Lenin, refer to them, look to them for inspiration and follow in their intellectual footsteps? That the overwhelming majority should do so requires as an explanation more than simply the intrinsic worth or appeal of Marxism. Why Marx?

The answer is multiple; it is political as well as historical. Classical Marxism was a doctrine of revolution. It was critical of bourgeois capitalist society and made a claim to scientific knowledge about society's development. Without doubt Marx was a genius. It is not strange that he had followers and that his theories were taken up in Russia, as well as elsewhere. In the 1880's Russian intellectuals and revolutionaries found themselves without a coherent doctrine. They had lived through their period of intellectual nihilism and their abortive attempts to "return to the people." Conditions were ripe for a new doctrine, and Marxism fulfilled all their needs. Its roots were in many ways similar to the roots of the Westernizing tradition that had been current in Russia from the 1840's. It was materialistic, humanistic, and messianic. Most importantly, Marxism provided a more comprehensive theoretical framework than the Russian intellectuals had had up to that time.

Lenin was a convinced and devoted Marxist. He accepted the works of Engels as one with those of Marx and quoted them frequently and with authority as the last word in a dispute. But Marx and Engels were Germans writing in England about the conditions in capitalist countries. Lenin was a Russian concerned with revolution in his still primarily agricultural country. He consequently adapted much of Marx to his own needs. Where Marx had spoken of a proletarian revolution, Lenin envisaged a revolution led by the proletariat which was to join forces with the peasants. Where Marx saw the revolution as arising spontaneously because of the plight of the proletariat, Lenin conceived of the proletariat as being led by a tightly organized group of professional revolutionists. The party led the proletariat, who in turn led the peasants; and the leaders of the party led the party. This was not Marx's idea of how the revolution would occur. Nor did he envisage it as taking place in Russia, without its also taking place in the industrialized countries of Europe. Lenin however led the successful October Revolution in Russia. The revolution did not spread; and its gains were consolidated where they were won. The revolution was Lenin's, not Marx's, though carried on in the name of Marx. Because he was a successful and charismatic leader, Lenin's words as well as his unqualified endorsement of Marx and Engels were taken over whole.

Once successful, the revolution had to be justified, the people had to be enlisted in social reconstruction, and guidelines for future development had to be established. The justification was found in Marx's condemnation of capitalism, private property, and exploitation. But specific guidelines for the future were virtually nonexistent in the writings of Marx and Engels. They spoke of a classless society in which there would be no private property, in which each person would be allowed his free all-round development, and in which society would operate according to the principle of "from each according to his ability, to each according to his need"; twice Marx had briefly mentioned the "dictatorship of the proletariat" which Lenin in *The State and Revolution* claimed was a central tenet of Marxism. But none of this had been worked out in any detail.

Faced with a successful revolution which had been carried on in Marx's name, the victors justified both the bloodletting of the revolution and the hardships which the Russian people would have to endure in terms of Marxist theory. They then extended it to justify their own social reconstruction. Marxism was given official backing by the successful bolsheviks who had seized power. University posts were filled with Marxists who replaced the many non-Marxist scholars who were exiled.

Marxism thus became the official ideology of the leaders of the new Soviet state, an ideology which they propagated widely among the Soviet people. As an ideology Marxism was to serve three major and a number of minor functions. 1) It was to serve as a coherent world view for the Soviet people, replacing religion and any philosophical views they might hold; it was to provide the people with a single and new set of values. 2) It was to justify the policies of the new regime, give them a moral sanction, and make them acceptable to the Soviet people. 3) It was to infuse and guide the development of the society as a whole, and the actions of both leaders and ordinary citizens.

In this latter function Marxism provided the broad goal of communism as the end to be achieved by society. This end gave or was to give meaning to the actions of leaders and followers alike. It guided policy since it was in terms of the end that specific means were chosen. The more elaborate a theory and the more fully an end is described, the more guidance it gives in the choice of means. Where Marx's description of communism was found lacking, Lenin and others supplied norms of action. The end of communism as it was and is conceived by the Soviet leaders explains in large part the resolute abolition of private property and the violent elimination of the kulaks—the comparatively wealthy peasants—as a class, since communism is said to be possible only in a society without private property, without classes, and so without exploiters. That the kulaks had to be eliminated in the bloody way that Stalin chose is doubtful; yet even in Khrushchev's denouncement of Stalin's crimes this was not one of the sins mentioned—it was presumably accepted as being justified by the necessity of achieving a classless society.

The importance of theory in guiding practice has a long tradition in Marxism. Lenin for instance in a letter written to the journal *Under the Banner of Marxism* in 1922 says,

"without a solid philosophic grounding . . . no materialism . . .
can hold its own in this struggle and carry it through to the
end with complete success."[2] Stalin repeated Lenin's remark
that "Without a revolutionary theory there can be no revolutionary movement."[3] Khrushchev again and again stressed the
importance of Marxist-Leninist theory to practice. And on the
fiftieth anniversary of the Bolshevik Revolution a statement
issued by the CPSU read: "The experience of the past fifty
years has demonstrated that the strength of the communist
movement rests on its loyalty to Marxism-Leninism. The most
urgent task of the international communist movement is to
ensure its unity on the basis of Marxist-Leninist principles."[4]

While in a democracy the impetus for àction may come
from below and be guided by a plurality of theories, ends,
and aims, in the Soviet regime there is room for only one
theory, for one guiding theoretical framework, for one blueprint of society.

Though Marxist theory may and probably often does justify
the actions of the leaders to themselves, it is more significantly
used by the leaders to justify the regime's actions to the people, thereby helping to gain and keep their support. It explains
and justifies—at least to some extent—the sufferings and abuses
and sacrifices of the people. And the greater the abuses, the
greater is the justification required.

Because of the ideological uses to which it was put, Marxism,
and later Marxism-Leninism, became wedded to the leaders,
organizations, operation, and ultimately to some extent to the
people of the Soviet Union. Since the bolshevik revolutionaries
waved the banner of Marx and since the Soviet Union has been
nominally built on the foundation of Marxism and Leninism,
present leaders and thinkers cannot repudiate Marx without
repudiating their society. For them to do so would be similar
to an American's repudiating George Washington or the Declaration of Independence or the Constitution—though fortunately none of these extends into all the domains into which
Marxism-Leninism extends at its broadest.

In a like way, when communist parties became established
in the countries of Eastern Europe they brought with them the

ideology of Marxism-Leninism on the Soviet pattern. As Lenin changed or modified Marxism to the situation and needs in Russia, so Marxism-Leninism has been and is being modified according to the situation and national needs in Poland, Yugoslavia, or Hungary. Just as the Soviet theorists cannot repudiate Marx without repudiating their society, so theorists in the other countries of Eastern Europe cannot repudiate him without repudiating their regimes and societies.

When we realize that many of the present-day Marxists were raised on Marxism, trained in it at the universities and that they imbibed it almost daily in every form of literature, theatre, press, textbook, and so on, it is not surprising that they are Marxists, any more than it would be surprising to find that someone trained in American schools is a positivist or pragmatist. Because theory is so closely related to the social structure and life of the countries of Eastern Europe, devotion to Marx is fostered even more. This does not mean that Marx, Engels, or Lenin has to be swallowed whole. There are different interpretations of Marx and Lenin flourishing among the new Marxists. Some Marxists go so far as to be hardly recognizable as such, and seem closer to if not identical with positivists or pragmatists. Yet they claim to be Marxists and adhere to the view that socialism is preferable to capitalism and that communism—though variously interpreted—is the moral end worthy of achievement by mankind.

The new Marxists want socialism, not capitalism; they are loyal to their countries. When they are critical of their regimes or of governmental practices it is not despite Marx but more often because of Marx and in his name, claiming that the leaders have misread him or are unfaithful to his spirit. One of the characteristics of the new Marxists is that, unlike the old Marxist-Leninists of the Stalinist era, one can no longer be sure what they will say.

In explaining why East European thinkers are Marxist we should also remember that in the USSR and in many of the other countries of Eastern Europe the Government owns and controls the publishing houses and sees to it that only Marxist works are published. If others are written—and the very writing of such works in some cases may be dangerous—they never emerge from the drawers of the authors.

Politics and history help us to see why Marx reigns; at the same time we cannot deny the inherent attractions of Marxism itself. Its claim to be scientific, to have uncovered the laws of historical and social development, lends it prestige. According to these laws it claims that socialism and communism are the heirs of the future, and that their triumph over dying capitalism is inevitable. It puts Marxists on the winning side. It also claims moral superiority over capitalism, since it claims to do away with the sources of exploitation, oppression, and social injustice which it identifies with capitalism. It is this-worldly, offering hope of an ideal society in the perhaps-not-too-far-distant future. It also consoles the have-nots, claiming that their ills, misery, and misfortune are not of their own doing but the result of their being exploited, robbed, and taken advantage of by imperialist powers, by the rich and powerful. Small wonder that this has such appeal to the underdeveloped countries of the world.

Though Marxism cannot be given up without giving up the revolution and the aims of and justification for the existing socialist order, Marx and Engels left much unsaid, including what communism means in detail and how it can be achieved. The new Marxists by no means repudiate Marx. Within the Marxist system they interpret and theorize to the extent that their leaders allow. Where they criticize the existing regimes or their policies, they do so in the name of the values espoused and expounded by Marx. Where they are most free and creative, however, is in those areas where Marx is least explicit or had little, if anything, to say.

The Amorphous Essence of Marxism

The Marxism which Marx left as a legacy was amorphous. He left no systematic body of doctrine and no unified presentation of his thought. What his followers found themselves with was a vast array of articles and speeches, published books, unfinished material for three additional volumes of *Capital*, letters, and the early manuscripts which were largely ignored until published as the first volumes of a projected collection of the works of Marx and Engels. From this unsystematic mass of material, commentators and self-styled Marxists could and still can pick and choose.

Engels in his book *Anti-Dühring* presented a systematic account of Marxism and divided it into three major areas: philosophy, political economy, and socialism. But many Marxist purists balk at calling this account Marxist because it contains a good deal that is original with Engels, especially in philosophy, where he extended the notion of dialectics to all of nature and natural science. Lenin in his summaries of Marxism generally follows the division of Engels though he treats the tactics of the class struggle of the proletariat as distinct from socialism. Contemporary Marxism-Leninism is divided into five branches. The first two, which make up the philosophical foundations of Marxism, are called dialectical materialism and historical materialism. The third branch consists of the critique of the political economy of capitalism, the fourth of the theory and tactics of the international communist movement, and the fifth of the theory of socialism and communism, sometimes referred to as scientific socialism or scientific communism.

Marxism cannot be reduced to a set of a few propositions without distorting it. The variety we find in the new Marxism comes from the amorphous heritage, from the accretions of Engels, Lenin, and others, and from the changing times, countries, and circumstances in which it has developed. There is scarcely a single doctrine that all Marxists would agree on, and certainly none that is peculiar to Marxism alone. All of the new Marxists at least nominally acknowledge Marx as their intellectual forefather; some also acknowledge Engels and Lenin, and a few even acknowledge Stalin. Where a large majority hold a certain set of propositions in common, the interpretations which they give to them are not necessarily identical. The new Marxists differ among themselves as to whom to recognize as their authority or authorities, what to accept and what to change from these authorities, and how to interpret—and, if appropriate, apply—what they accept. They disagree on what needs to be added to make the position

complete or presently relevant. Despite these differences, however, a brief inventory of some of the generally acknowledged
major tenets of classical Marxism and an indication of some of
the major changes in Marxism is not amiss here.

A central factor of Marxism, which supplied much of its
dynamism and its appeal, is its *social criticism*. Young Marx
had a view of contemporary man and of his plight, which he
modified but never lost throughout his life. Whether he referred to it as oppression, as alienation, or as exploitation, he
was keenly aware of man's inhumanity to man. As a consequence he recognized the need of changing society, and not
merely reinterpreting it.

Marx's analysis early led him to a *theory of classes*. The
fragmentation of man in the society in which Marx lived, his
alienation, and his exploitation, Marx claimed, were bound up
with the fact that society was divided into two major and hos-
tile classes—a fact which Marx found characteristic of the historical development of man ever since he left primitive communal societies. It was clear in the slave-holding societies, in
feudal society, and in capitalist society. In each instance one
class was dominant, the other dominated. The division was
closely bound up with the division of labor according to which
men specialized and fragmented their productive activities,
instead of enjoying the full, all-round development of their
capacities. And together with division of labor came private
property which similarly divided man from man and further
led men to subjugate and exploit other men.

The triple evil of alienation, division of labor, and exploitation went together with class society and all could only be
done away with together. This called for a *revolution*. The
members of the dominant class would never willingly give up
their property and their dominant position. They must be forced
to do this. But they must be forced to do so not by some group
which would in turn place itself above others. The solution
for Marx was that the revolution, if it was to successfully end
exploitation, class society, division of labor, and private property, must be carried out by some group or class which morally
represented all of mankind: all men would govern themselves,

and without division into classes or exploitation, all could share in the common goods of the earth and of society. In Marx's view, the only class capable of carrying out such a revolution was the proletariat, which in fact represented all of working mankind, had no property interests, and had nothing to lose but its chains.

The result of the revolution would be the establishment of socialism, which would be a transition period to *communism*. Communist society would be free of exploitation, alienation, private property, and oppression, it would be classless and each person would be allowed the fullest development of which he was capable. He would contribute to society according to his ability and receive from society according to his need.

Despite Marxism's morally motivated critique of existing society and its theoretical justification of revolution, its ideal of communism could not be made acceptable so long as it remained purely theoretical. To save it from being simply another utopian theory, to make it scientific, it had to be grounded in the real world and be shown to be one with it. That it was so grounded Marx thought he had shown in his interpretation of history and his economic theory.

Strongly influenced by Hegel, Marx held on to dialectics; but placing Hegel on his feet, he adopted what he called materialism. *Dialectics* meant several things for Marx and expressed a number of his insights into the working of the world. As Hegelian dialectics emphasized the essential change, interrelation, and antagonism in the development of the Absolute, so Marx found and emphasized the factors of change, interrelation, and antagonism in society and its development. Man was an active doer and knower who was dynamically interrelated with other men and nature. He found himself in a society which contained contradictions, antagonisms, and opposition; and he helped change his society by working out these oppositions and antagonisms which were the moving force of change in society. Engels extended the theory of dialectics to all of nature, explicitly developing general laws of dialectics which were exemplified in all realms of reality—nature and natural science, society, history, and human thought. Whether Marx would have agreed with this extension is a much disputed point.

For Marx, however, dialectics did not operate abstractly. His materialism expressed itself in his belief that it is not ideas that change the world. The world can only be changed by changing actual conditions. Religion, philosophy, political theory, institutions are not the fundamental factors in a society, but make up the *superstructure* of a society. They reflect the *economic base* of society and change as it changes. Consciousness does not determine life, but life determines consciousness. In this sense man's practical activities, the way he produces and what he produces, are more important than his theories and ideologies or the representations and misrepresentations of what he does. His practical life forces certain social relations and institutions, certain laws and theories upon him, despite the rationalizations and reasons he may give in their defense. Slavery was justified as long as it was economically necessary and profitable. Only after it became relatively unprofitable in comparison with other productive relations was it condemned in the name not of production but of morality. Morality, however, just like other forms of ideology, is determined ultimately by the economic conditions of society, which are primary. As these conditions change, they bring with them other social and ideological changes.

Generalizations based on this view lead to three Marxist claims: 1) that history is determined in its development by the development of its economic base; 2) that the laws of history—and Marx assumed both that there were such laws and that in general they led to the progressive development of mankind—could be found by uncovering the laws of economic development; and 3) that a proletarian revolution could be effective only if it resulted in changing the economic conditions of society in accordance with the laws of its development. These led Marx to his intensive study of the political economy of capitalism.

Marx developed his *labor theory of value* as the basis of his economic analysis of capitalism. According to this the value of a commodity is determined by the amount of simple social labor time required for its production. However, in capitalist society there is one item which is not sold at its real value, and this is man's labor. The owners of the means of production, the industrialists, hire laborers and pay them not the equivalent of what they produce but the lowest wage possible which will still keep them alive. The difference between what the worker is paid and the value of what he produces represents *surplus value* or the profit of the owner. The owners of the means of production therefore acquire their wealth by exploiting, or robbing, their workers. Their greed leads them to greater and greater exploitation and pushes the growing army of labor into greater and greater poverty. The antagonism between the capitalist and the worker is one expression of the contradictions in capitalism. The contradiction between communal production and private ownership can be overcome only by getting rid of private ownership. But the capitalists will give up their property and position only when forced to. By exploiting the workers to an ever greater extent, however, they will eventually force the workers to revolt in order to stay alive. They will force the proletariat to seize the means of production, to do away with classes and private property, to rid the world of exploitation and the oppression of man by man. The result will be the establishment of a classless communist society.

What we saw initially as a desirable product of Marx's social critique is now shown to be its necessary result: the doom of capitalism and the ultimate triumph of communism are said to be inevitable because of the contradictions present in capitalism and because of the laws of historical development. Yet to be successful the revolution would have to take place in a highly industrialized society, for only in such a society is there sufficient wealth necessary to satisfy the needs of all; it would have to take place in a country with a large, impoverished proletariat, since only there would the masses be forced to revolt and overcome the contradiction between social production and private ownership; and the revolution would have to be worldwide in effect, otherwise the capitalist forces in those countries where the revolution did not take place would attack and undermine the revolutionaries to protect themselves and their property and position.

Marxism and Revisionism

What remains and what does not of this inheritance? What has been kept, with or without reinterpretation? What has been tacitly dropped or revised? What has been added?

According to the official Soviet Marxist-Leninist position, all the writings of Marx, Engels, and Lenin are correct, true, and valid. Where they differ, they differ only because of changing times and differing applications. In the Soviet Union the Communist Party leaders are the guardians of orthodoxy and doctrinal purity, and they decide which interpretations of the classical Marxist writers are orthodox and which are not. Those that are not orthodox are called revisionist, and condemned. The term "revisionist" was applied originally to Eduard Bernstein (1850–1932), a German Social Democrat who argued that Marx was in part mistaken in his theories and had to be revised. By extension, any position which attempted to change the doctrines of Marx and Engels by rejecting and correcting certain of their claims came to be called revisionist. What constitutes rejection and correction as opposed to creative reinterpretation, however, is often a matter of bitter dispute. The term "revisionist" consequently now makes sense only with respect to a body of orthodox interpretation, where orthodoxy is decided by those holding political power. What the Communist Party of Poland may claim is revisionist and condemn might well be considered orthodox and non-revisionist by the Communist Party of Yugoslavia. The official and therefore orthodox Marxism-Leninism of the Soviet Union is branded revisionist by the Chinese. Since the Chinese have no political power over the Soviet Union, however, they have no effective means of enforcing their interpretation of orthodoxy outside of their own domain.

In all the East European countries which we will consider there are touchstones of orthodoxy. In some of the countries more latitude of interpretation and discussion is allowed than in others. But in all of them there is an official or quasi-official interpretation which is expressed in the textbooks and press, in public information and propaganda media. The new Marxism operates within this framework.

What remains of Marx's theory—subject to varying interpretations—is his social critique of capitalism, his denunciation of private property and exploitation, his social dialectic, his economic approach to history, and his vision of a classless, communist society. His views on alienation and the division of labor are creating much controversy, since many now hold that though their extreme forms disappear along with capitalism, they may take new forms which are appearing in socialism.

Marx's basic orientation, his approach to history, and his moral ideal of communism have remained. The details of his theory and some of its major components, however, have either been dropped or so radically reinterpreted as to be almost unrecognizable. The chief change has occurred with regard to Marx's view of the revolution—both what kind it should be and how it should be achieved. By the turn of the century it had become clear that the proletariat was not getting poorer and poorer, but that its lot was improving. Lenin introduced many changes in Marxian revolutionary theory. According to him the revolution would not be carried out spontaneously by the proletariat but would be led by professional revolutionists, who would be organized secretly; they would lead the proletariat, who would in turn lead the peasants. The revolution would take place not in the highly industrialized and advanced capitalist countries but in the less developed countries, which formed the weakest link in the capitalist chain.

Marx's economic theory has fared equally poorly. His labor theory of value proved unequal to the task of describing the complexity of capitalist economics. Though the demise of capitalism is still awaited and private profit equated with exploitation, Marx's economic laws are no longer much mentioned or defended. Lenin shifted the focus from the exploitation of the proletariat to the exploitation of colonies in the age of imperialism. It was not the workers but the colonies which were to inaugurate communism. This meant that communism could not longer be held to be possible only if achieved on a worldwide scale, and only in the highly industrialized societies.

Marx had seen his laws as working themselves out with inexorable necessity; in Lenin's hands they became quasi-voluntary. Strict historical determinism, which had been associated with Marx's views by many of his early followers, was replaced by the notion of historical trends; and emphasis was shifted from the necessity of history's development to the necessity of man's acting. In the new stage of socialism, moreover, the base no longer determines the superstructure in the way it does or was supposed to have done in capitalist society. The superstructure and in particular the communist party, it is claimed, can influence and help determine the development of the economic base.

Additions to Marxism since Marx's day form a growing portion of the new Marxism. In philosophy Marx and Engels had left at best a sketchy system. The dialectical materialism of Engels, while part of the official Soviet Marxism-Leninism, is by no means agreed upon in detail. Lenin added a "copy" theory of knowledge to Marxism, which also is not without its difficulties. The meaning of "materialism" and "matter" are undergoing scrutiny. And while Marx had at best only an implicit ethics, a full-fledged ethics is now developing. The Soviet philosopher E. V. Il'enkov noted recently that "It is indisputable that in the Marxist literature of the last ten years one can observe a heightened interest in the problems of personality and individuality, in the problem of a human being as the subject of the historical process, in the problem of 'reification' and 'de-reification,' and in general, in that entire gamut of questions connected in one way or another with an analysis of human activity and its conditions. . . ."[5] These are problems which if not entirely new to Marxism are receiving their first detailed contemporary development.

In the realm of politics the Leninist-Stalinist doctrine of socialism in one country has been extended into the doctrine that there are many roads to socialism. The political hegemony of the Communist Party of the Soviet Union has been questioned. The Leninist addition to Marxism of a doctrine of the party and partisanship brought with it later claims about the party's omnicompetence. While leadership of the party in communist countries is still a matter of doctrine, its omnicompetence in a few realms (e.g., the arts and science) has been challenged, not entirely successfully in the Soviet Union, more successfully in Yugoslavia, Poland, and Czechoslovakia. The doctrine of peaceful coexistence is a concession to the nuclear age. Militant atheism, never advocated by Marx, has been in and out of favor in the Soviet Union and Eastern Europe over the years. Poland's traditional Catholicism has made for more toleration of religion in communist doctrine in Poland than we find in the Marxist line in the Soviet Union.

The broad area of scientific communism is another accretion to Marxist theory. The positive content of communism was not Marx's concern. Nor, as a future state of affairs, was it within his grasp to describe. But the establishment of socialism—even in one country—and the Soviet Union's drive toward building communism raised for Soviet theoreticians and politicians the necessity of forging a coherent doctrine of communism which could serve to guide and motivate the communist builders of the future society. Uncovering the laws of socialist development calls for the genius of a Marx. While this genius has not yet been found, scientific communism has nonetheless been added to the body of official Marxist and Marxist-Leninist doctrine and concern.

In the light of these manifold revisions the question of when Marxism ceases to be Marxism remains a moot point.

Present Divergent Trends

The new Marxism is so diverse that it cannot be easily or neatly divided and categorized. But Marxism has always had within it certain tensions which have caused recurring differences of emphasis; and the union of Marxist theory with political power has caused other tensions which have also led to recurring divisions, still present today.

We have seen that Marxism was historically allied with the Bolshevik Revolution and that Marxism thereafter became an ideology used in the service of the leaders of the Soviet Union. As an ideology it became formulated into a more or less coherent doctrine which was widely taught and preached, and which was to be learned and accepted, not questioned. Under Stalin innovation was taboo, except when and how he permitted. Those in charge of education and propaganda produced books and pamphlets, student texts, agitator manuals, and instructive material for all levels from the simplest summaries to university textbooks.

The Soviet Union thus produced a large number of ideologists and an even larger number of hacks. The latter repeated and simplified what they were told. The former served as a link between the political leaders and the people, including the intelligentsia, guiding and controlling the latter as much as they could. Their job was to defend and explain the Soviet way of life and Soviet policies. Their end was to motivate action and to guard the status quo. They appealed to the emotions as well as to reason, and to authority even in the face of reason. An ideologist is a theoretician, but one whose primary allegiance is to the system he is defending, not to abstract truth or the logical clarity or coherence of the system. Soviet ideologists and Marxist ideologists in other East European countries form one group of thinkers. They are closely tied to the political scene and act as spokesmen for the leaders of the country. They represent the official party line and lay it down to those who wander too far afield in literature, the arts, philosophy, economics, and other areas. They issue party directives, watch out for the cultural purity of social life, and expel those like L. Kolakowski in Poland, whom they consider to have gone too far. They are in at least one sense new Marxists, for Marx certainly never envisaged his doctrine as being a dogma imposed from above.

But not all Marxist theoreticians are ideologists, and a split has developed between the ideologists who sacrifice logic to party needs and those Marxists who wish to abide by the demands of intellectual honesty and who are concerned with rendering the terms of Marxism systematically clear and unambiguous. Members of the latter group are interested in clarifying the statements repeated by rote by the ideologists, they are concerned with analyzing the meanings of terms and the logical consistency of statements within the system, they attempt to test the validity of empirical claims against reality, and they are anxious either to fill in the vast holes and areas left untouched by Marx or to experiment with new ideas and approaches—even while acknowledging the essential correctness of Marxism. These new Marxists do not form a single group, nor are they necessarily adventuresome or inquisitive in all domains. They can be clearly differentiated from the ideologists, with whom they are often at odds within the Marxist camp. But they are themselves split by the ambiguous Marxist legacy they have inherited.

One of the basic tensions in Marxist theory from its inception has been between its professed materialism and its theory of dialectics. As a doctoral candidate Marx was a follower of Hegel and wrote his doctoral dissertation in philosophy in the Hegelian style. Though he later threw over Hegel's idealistic philosophy, he never gave up dialectics. He was converted to what he called materialism and claimed to have turned Hegel off his head, putting him on his feet. The inversion consisted in part of the claim that it is not ideas which make history, but that ideas are the result of man's economic (in Marx's terms "material") life. Men think the way they do because they live the way they do. Despite Marx's insistence on the primacy of man's economic life over his intellectual life, he also claimed that society and history did indeed progress dialectically, as a result of tensions or contradictions, which were overcome, only to lead to further tensions. Whether or not Marx held that all of nature as well as society and history operates dialectically is a moot point. But Engels made explicit the doctrine that all of reality is governed by dialectical laws, leading to the doctrine known as dialectical materialism.

The union of dialectics and materialism from the start, however, has been shaky. And Marxists both in the nineteenth century and in the 1920's in Russia have disagreed as to how to unite the two and have split into those materialists who claim that dialectics is a Hegelian mystification which is to be analyzed away in favor of a consistent materialism and those dialecticians who emphasize dialectics, claiming that without it materialism sinks into a vulgar mechanism, unable to account for knowledge, man's activity, or the supposed contradictions found in nature. Both trends are represented among the new Marxists as they raise again the disputes which were peremptorily settled by Stalin's fiat in 1931.

Closely related to this is another dispute which divides Marxists in Eastern Europe. It centers on the relation between the early writings of Marx, which were philosophical, humanistic, and posthumously published, and those of his later life, whether taken in conjunction with those of Engels or not. The dispute is between those humanists who emphasize the young Marx and his humanism—his concern for the plight of mankind, his views of man, his anthropology and depiction of alienation—and the scientific socialists who emphasize the older Marx and the scientific aspects characteristic of *Capital*. The dispute also involves the question of whether Engels is to be treated as speaking for Marx, or whether Marx's materialistic interpretation of history is to be preserved inviolate from Engel's formulation of it. In the Soviet Union the equation of Marx and Engels is still the official line; in Poland each position has its spokesmen; in Yugoslavia the humanists seem to hold the field.

Another division, also dating from the end of the nineteenth century, is based on differing interpretations of man's role in history. One school, emphasizing the determinism of history, argued that when conditions were right the revolution would take place and socialism and communism would follow. The laws of economics and of history work themselves out with iron necessity. At best one could help ease the birth pangs of the new society. The other group in contrast, though using much the same language, argued that man must make his history within his given conditions; Lenin led the activist pack, arguing that the revolution would not come spontaneously among the workers, but that when conditions were ripe the revolution had to be led by those who were ready to do so. The revolution could not succeed if conditions were not right, but neither could it take place, even given the right conditions, unless the revolutionists were on hand to seize the moment. Lenin's activist interpretation of history is dominant at present, and forms one of the clearer and more generally accepted tenets of the new Marxists. But how freedom is to be interpreted and how determinism is to be handled within Marxism remain open questions.

A fourth factor in Marxism which has led to different emphases and interpretations is the tension between Marx's critical and his constructive thought. Most of Marx's efforts were concerned with criticizing capitalist society and the capitalist economic system in particular. He wished to change society, for he saw it as badly in need of change. An acid critic, he was also a revolutionary; he not only called on the proletariat to revolt and seize the means of production, but predicted that they would do so. Absorbed by his research into the laws of capitalist economy and embroiled in the labor movement, Marx gave little thought to the establishment of communism. This would take care of itself once conditions were changed. But since he left so little to guide the builders of communism, they have had to fend for themselves.

Once the means of production were seized by the state, conditions did not automatically change. The proper means to be taken to reach socialism and communism have had to be worked out and are still being worked out. And there is no lack of disagreement as to which means are the best and just what the goal of communism means in detail. The ideologists and some of the theoreticians are forging plans and outlining actions geared to reach communism in the foreseeable future.

But the critical aspect of Marxism is not so easily silenced. And new Marxists, in the name of Marx, are questioning both whether the vision of party leaders is actually that of communism rather than of some distortion of it, and whether they are choosing the most efficacious means to achieve their ends. The amount of criticism tolerated varies from country to country. But the critical aspect of Marxism supplies an orthodox cover for loyally dissenting Marxists.

According to Marx communism could succeed only if it was worldwide. The doctrine of socialism-in-one-country grew as a result of the success of the Bolshevik Revolution and the failure of the revolution to spread to Germany and other countries. But if communism could be realized only on a worldwide scale, could the Bolshevik Revolution be called a communist revolution and could the society that developed in the Soviet Union be called either socialist or communist?

The dispute over whether Russia should export revolution to other countries at the risk of what had been won, or whether it should first consolidate its gains and only secondarily seek to foment revolution elsewhere raged in the twenties, was temporarily settled by Stalin's triumph over Trotsky, but once again divides Marxists today. Can the Soviets be called Marxists if they are more concerned with raising the standard of living of their people than with aiding the less wealthy socialist countries or with actively precipitating revolution? Those Marxists who side with the Chinese think not, and here they may well be more Marxist than the Soviets—though Marx never thought of either Russia or China as the seat of communism, nor of communism as anything other than worldwide. It was Trotsky's and Lenin's innovation that communist revolutions would take place not in the most advanced capitalist countries but in the most backward countries governed by the capitalists, since these formed the weakest link in the chain of capitalism. The "exportists" still debate with the consolidationists, though it is doubtful whether either of these new Marxists would have had Marx's blessing.

This dispute is not far removed from another one which divides Marxists. Internationalism expresses itself not only on the level of revolution but also on the level of humanism. And here some of the humanists are at odds with the nationalists. Marxism changed when it was applied in Russia. It changed again when applied in China. Similarly it changes with each country and is adapted to the conditions, history, and needs of the country and its people. The hegemony of the USSR has been challenged by China, by Yugoslavia, and to a lesser extent by Poland and Hungary among others. But is Marxist doctrine one or many? Does it teach the way to socialism and betterment in individual countries or to all workers, to all men? Many Marxist humanists argue for the universal application of Marx's critique of exploitation and oppression; the nationalists emphasize that each country should and must move to socialism and to communism at its own rate and in its own way.

The debate on decentralization or centralism strikes at the heart of the administrative and economic organization of socialist society. Some Yugoslavs are especially vocal on this issue, arguing for worker's cooperatives in which the workers of a factory share both in its policy decisions and in its profits. They insist that this and not state capitalism is in the spirit of true Marxism. The state can only wither away when the workers are allowed to handle and actually do handle all their own affairs.

These and other issues split the new Marxists. Nor are the issues themselves clear-cut. They overlap and often shade into one another, and someone holding one position on one issue is not thereby forced to hold a particular position on the other issues. Both a humanist Marxist and a scientific socialist, as we have characterized them, may be either a nationalist or an internationalist, a critical or a constructive Marxist, a determinist or an activist, a dialectician or a materialist. Which position or combination of them is true Marxism? Each can go to Marx's writings for support. Each is Marxism and none is; and insofar as they are the products of living twentieth-century Marxist thought each goes back to Marx, selects from him, and surpasses him. The new Marxism is a varied and living body of thought. Its content and significance form the nucleus of the chapters which follow.

2

Marxist Prophecy and Communist Inevitability

■ Was Marx a prophet, foretelling the future, or a scholar, scientifically predicting a necessary series of events completely knowable on the basis of present evidence? Or was he neither of these and simply a gifted observer engaged in acute description? Marxist and non-Marxist interpreters of Marx's writings differ considerably in their answers to these questions.

If central to Marx's writings was the claim that the lot of the proletarians would continually deteriorate until, on the brink of starvation, they would be forced by their condition to revolt, to seize the means of production, and to establish a worldwide socialist or communist system beginning in the most highly advanced industrialized countries, then Marx was simply mistaken. The critics of Marx would here be correct. But though there are texts of Marx which support such claims, present-day Marxists do not accept such facile refutations of Marxism. For them the heart of the Marxist position does not stand or fall with specific statements of supposed predictions. The inherent evil of capitalism, its internal contradictions, its inevitable downfall, and the eventual worldwide triumph of socialism carry no specific deadlines. Marx was correct, they claim, in describing capitalism and the general trend of its development—the periodic depressions which did take place after Marx wrote *Capital*, the growth of large industry at the expense of the small, the world-character of competition, the outbreak of world war among the capitalist countries, the rise and spread of socialism, and the decline of capitalism. And Marx was able to foretell all this because of his scientific analysis of capitalism.

In some ways Marx did too good a job. His description of the evils of capitalism and his claims concerning the necessity of its decay because of its internal contradictions remain the general position repeated and believed by new as well as old Marxists. His condemnations of capitalism and his statement of the laws of its development have not been changed since his own day, except for a few modifications introduced by Lenin.

According to the Marxist analysis, as we have seen, capitalists make their profit only by exploiting the workers, paying them less than the value they produce and pocketing the excess of surplus value for themselves. Motivated by an insatiable thirst for greater and greater profit, the capitalist squeezes out of the workers as much work for as little pay as he can. He may make temporary compromises and give in to the workers if forced, as he has done during the hundred years since the appearance of *Capital*. But such delaying tactics do not change the essence of the capitalist system. They prolong its life; but they cannot rejuvenate it. Capitalism is necessarily built on the exploitation of the workers. It needs constantly expanding markets and to get them it must either move into less developed lands or feed on the destruction of war and the ploy of built-in obsolescense. Its production is completely socialized. Its ownership is private. This is its basic contradiction. The owners of production get richer and richer and also fewer and fewer in number. The necessary and unavoidable outcome is that ownership must eventually be socialized and pass from the hands of the few to those of the workers.

The more sophisticated Marxists realize that conditions in the West have changed to some extent since Marx's day. But even they consider the changes as superficial, not as basic or as invalidating the essential Marxist critique of capitalism. The relative affluence of workers in advanced industrial countries such as the United States is thus for the new Marxists no argument against Marx or his thought. The owners of the means of production have found that the best way to survive is to take less and give the worker more. They have also expanded their exploitation to include the underdeveloped countries of the world, whether they be present or former colonies. They have preserved their wealth through continued expansion. But the workers are by no means as well-off as they should be, the poor and needy are still numerous, and the system remains basically unjust.

Marx claimed to have uncovered the laws of the development of capitalism and to have described them in his economic works. Even more importantly he claimed to have uncovered the key to historical development. His materialist interpretation of history applies not only to the capitalist era, but to the earlier periods of historical development as well. Here again Marx wrote perhaps too well. For his position has been too slavishly followed by his successors. It has to a large extent been dogmatized and not developed.

The Base-Superstructure Relationship

The basic position is that the economic base of society determines the social superstructure built upon it. Social relations, politics, institutions, morality, philosophy, art, and religion are all determined ultimately by the economic conditions of a society. Man must produce and keep himself alive before he can engage in theorizing about his activity, justifying or explaining it. The way he produces and what he produces determine the way he organizes his life. This in turn ultimately determines his thoughts and his theories about life. As his conditions change, so his thinking changes. In a class society, moreover, the leaders of the society propagate their own views through the schools, churches, and press which aim at justifying and preserving the status quo. By this means they attempt to preserve their status and wealth. Private property becomes sacrosanct and theft a heinous crime. The oppressed are taught the ideology of the rulers, and they live in a society governed by the laws of the rulers and enforced by the police and other state instruments of oppression. For the state is the institutionalized representative of the rulers. The workers, however, are forced sooner or later by their condition of life to see through the myths they are taught. They come to develop their own views about justice, freedom, equality, and the like, which form the heritage of the proletariat and which will eventually be realized in a classless society.

The attractive simplicity of the materialist interpretation of history, however, is deceptive. That man must live before he can think would be denied by no one. But the task of showing that economic conditions determine ideas and that economic conditions are ultimately the moving force in history is easier to enunciate than to prove, demonstrate, or even illustrate. If these notions are the core of Marxism, then the unfilled task of later Marxists should have been to complete in detail the picture which Marx had sketched out in broad strokes. Few, if any, of the new Marxists seem inclined to this tedious task, though they have made a few additions to the doctrine in order to handle its more obvious shortcomings.

One addition is the doctrine of the relative independence of the various parts of the superstructure. The institutions and ideas of a class or society, it is held, are determined ultimately by the economic conditions of that society. But this does not mean that if one knows a society's economic conditions he can deduce its social relations, institutions, or ideas. For these are in part determined by other factors. A great many accidental and incidental events, which do not radically change or effect the elements of the superstructure, do tend to modify it. Elements of the superstructure, each ultimately determined by the economic conditions, also tend to influence one another. And each element has its own peculiar form partially because of the way it historically developed. The morality of a certain age, for example, depends ultimately on the economic conditions of the age, but partially on the morality of the preceding age, on the religious beliefs held, on the legal system and institutions, and so on.

Added to the relative independence of the elements of the superstructure is the doctrine of the "lag of social consciousness behind social being." This maintains that changes in the base are not reflected directly and immediately by changes in the superstructure. The latter changes more slowly than the former and the superstructure has a certain inertia of its own. People tend to continue in their old habits and beliefs, even when the reasons for holding these beliefs or following these habits have changed. It takes time for the old to be replaced by the useful new—a fact which accounts in part for the difference between generations in a developing society and for the "remnants or survivals of capitalism" which are still to be found in socialist society.

The addition of these modifications makes the theory more plausible. However, once it has been admitted that the base does not automatically and directly influence the superstructure, it is still necessary to demonstrate how it does exert its influence. The new Marxists show little inclination to carry through the analysis. They rest content, as their predecessors did, with claiming that the intervening links can be produced and that detailed analyses can be found in the writings of Marx or Lenin, and then simply asserting that, for instance, bourgeois philosophy is the result of decadent and dying bourgeois capitalism, that bourgeois morality represents the immorality of the capitalist system, and so on. It would be extremely enlightening for a Marxist to show how the philosophy of Bertrand Russell in its various periods, for example, is the result of changing economic conditions in England. But this is perhaps to ask for too much, for neither the old nor the new Marxists claim that the beliefs or actions of *individuals* can be explained by their thesis. They confine their theory to the beliefs and social relations of classes or masses. Yet even on this level, nothing has been forthcoming which shows in detail how any particular philosophical or religious system is determined by the economic conditions of a society. The investigation of the intervening links seems an obvious need in any developed Marxist system, but it is one that has not yet been undertaken.

The above additions tend to give a more reasonable account of the "determinism" of the base on the superstructure. But the very meaning of the terms "base" and "superstructure" are unclear and are being discussed and reinterpreted by contemporary Soviet Marxist philosophers.[1] The economic base of society was supposed to consist of the means and modes of production and the consequent relations of production. The superstructure was the social relations arising from the base and the social, political, legal, moral, intellectual, artistic, religious, and other aspects of life in a society. Stalin in his letters on Marxism and linguistics instituted one major change which has become incorporated into official Soviet doctrine. This maintains that though there is nothing intermediary between base and superstructure, not everything is covered by this dichotomy. Thus, for instance, language is part neither of the base nor of the superstructure. It falls outside of both, and is to some extent therefore independent of economic development. Similarly, it has been decided that mathematics, symbolic logic, and the facts of science all fall outside the dichotomy. They remain what they are independent of the economic base. The same mathematics and scientific facts can be and have been discovered by people in socialist and in capitalist society, and these, unlike political laws, morality, and social institutions, will not change because of different forms of ownership of the means of production.

The addition of a third sphere which falls outside of the base and the superstructure, however, simply complicated matters and does not solve the problem of adequately defining the terms making up the basic dichotomy. Are laws which affect industry and determine ways of production part of the base, or are they a part of the superstructure which inappropriately seems to influence the base instead of being influenced by it? Are inventions relating to production part of the base, part of the superstructure, or independent of both? Can "economic" conditions be separated from the mass of social conditions with which they are interwound so that one can clearly say what is influencing what? The critics of Marxism have claimed not; the new Marxists are struggling to clarify the issues, but again as yet without evident consensus or success.

The final aspect of the base-superstructure relation which we shall look at is the Stalinist doctrine of the active role of the superstructure. In classical Marxism the superstructure, if not completely passive, was certainly not one of the motive forces of society. The new Marxism, however, following Stalin, claims that in socialist society the superstructure can be an active—and even a motor—influence in the development of socialist society. The active force of the superstructure in pre-socialist society was and is precluded by the fact that in such societies the laws of social development are unknown, denied, or ignored. The society consequently develops blindly. By contrast, the laws of social development in socialist society are supposedly known, at least in part, and so can be consciously used in order to promote the natural and lawful development of society. The leaders of a socialist country cannot change the base whimsically or in any way they choose. But through organization, through planning (five year or longer plans), through moral, political, and economic stimulation of the workers the leaders can consciously guide their society along the road from socialism to communism. The way in which this is possible is closely linked with the new interpretation of the laws of history.

Determinism and the Laws of History

In *Capital* Marx wrote "Intrinsically, it is not a question of the higher degree of development of the social antagonisms that result from the natural laws of capitalist production. It is a question of these laws themselves, of these tendencies working with iron necessity towards inevitable results." [2] The quote is typical of Marx's writings and contains the seeds of two different interpretations. Those who seized upon the portion which indicates that the laws of capitalist production work with iron necessity compared them to laws of nature and insisted that history was *determined* in some strong sense of the term. The laws of economics determined the development of a society just as the laws of nature determined the action of physical bodies. At most, Marxist theory could bring to the consciousness of the proletariat the historical necessity of their revolt before it might otherwise have reached them. This might serve to hasten their revolution, to "shorten and lessen the birth-pangs." [3] But the revolution and its success were guaranteed by the laws of social development and could in no way be permanently hampered or avoided. In this sense it was inevitable.

Marx's use of the word "tendency" however gives ground for another and less strict interpretation of the development of history. If Marx's laws are simply tendencies, then they push society in a certain direction. This does not preclude the possibility that the direction may be modified by other pushes or pulls. *If* the tendency goes unchecked, *if* no counter-tendency intervenes, then the predicted result will be forthcoming. Developing the analogy of birth further, we can see that in a human birth man's intervention can hasten or ease the birth of a child, which follows a general rule or tendency or law. But we also know that in childbirth direct intervention—Caesarian section or other—is often required if the child is to be born alive. Could the tendency of capitalism to produce socialism be aborted? Could it produce a still-born?

It is quite clear that Lenin did not regard Marx as holding a fatalistic doctrine which implied that whatever happens would happen no matter what anyone did, or whether anyone acted at all. Instead, he held that without some kind of intervention the working class would arrive only at trade-union consciousness, and not at revolutionary consciousness. For the revolt to take place it must be brought about by a dedicated group of revolutionaries who would lead the masses. Without this group the revolution would not take place. He claimed that the laws of social development operate with a certain necessity, he spoke of the laws of history, of the inevitability of the decline of capitalism, and of the necessity of the triumph of socialism. But the necessity and inevitability were tempered by the requirement of active participation by a group at the appropriate moment. The revolution would not be produced spontaneously. It could not be produced at will. It required both the proper conditions in society and the active intervention of the revolutionaries.

Since Lenin's revolution was a success, his interpretation of determinism and of the inevitability of history prevails today so far as the transition from capitalism to socialism is concerned.

The present dominant Marxist position includes three claims. First, there are objective laws of history which determine, in some sense, its development. These laws are not strictly analogous to physical laws for they operate not independently of man's consciousness, but through man's consciousness. Man's motivations, however, are basically determined or formed by his economic circumstances. Therefore economic circumstances determine what he will do. To know the economic circumstances enables one to foresee how history will in general develop. Yet the laws are *tendencies* and as such are not as precise as some of the laws of physics are held to be; and mankind may not know *all* of the appropriate laws of economic—and therefore of historical—development. There may be unforeseen interventions of other laws which preclude the known law from operating freely and producing its natural result.

Secondly, the laws of history require the active intervention of man.[4] They operate through his consciousness, which can be influenced in such a way as to reinforce and speed up his activity in the direction of history's tendency. Though the position involves activism, it rejects an extreme voluntarism which would imply that man can do whatever he wants and that the direction of history depends primarily on man's will. Man can will to act in accord with the laws of history; if he chooses to act against them, he may retard their natural development, but he cannot effectively change it. His action is effective only to the extent that he considers the objective, economic, and other conditions of society.[5]

The third claim is that the decline of capitalism is inevitable since capitalism offers no hope for the progressive development of mankind. Socialism is inevitable because its development follows naturally from the development of capitalism and it alone offers mankind the hope of progressing morally and socially beyond capitalism. But nuclear warfare, among other things, has made it abundantly clear that mankind may not have a future, that it may in fact destroy itself. *If* mankind is to progress, it can do so only by moving on to socialism, and it is in this sense that socialism is now regarded as inevitable.

The New Laws of Social Development

Contemporary Soviet Marxists are unanimous in agreeing that the Bolshevik Revolution was Marxist and took place not only in Marx's name but in accordance with his theory. They claim that after a period of transition the Soviet Union became a socialist society and that it is now developing toward communism. After 1956 most Marxists were willing to admit that though some of what took place under Stalin was necessary, there were many abuses that were the result of the "personality cult" which grew up around him. They also admit that the road to communism is not an easy one. Mistakes are possible, trial and error are necessary, and eventual success will only be achieved by a patient struggle on the part of all the people.

The general laws of history are said to hold in socialist as well as in capitalist society. These include the law that the economic base of a society determines its social superstructure. Just as with any other society, the way to change Soviet society is to change its economic base. However, we are told, there are certain differences in the application of the general laws of social development in the case of the Soviet Union. The differences arise from the fact that the leaders of society are aware of the general laws of social development and use them to guide society's growth.

Two points are worth noting. The first is that under socialism, though the base is still the ultimately determining factor, the active role of the superstructure has become and will become increasingly important.[6] This supplies justification for the leadership of the communist party, for its primary role in the direction of society, and for its five-year and other plans. Its claim to greater knowledge is the basis for its leadership. While capitalist countries develop in a helter-skelter manner, the Soviet Union, it is claimed, is able to make progress because it is directed toward a specific end. In utilizing the insights of Marx and Lenin, its leaders can study the development of its economic base, channel this development, and so lay a firm foundation for the change of the superstructure.

Secondly, the new Marxism admits that socialism need not be a complete negation of capitalism, as some earlier Marxists had claimed it would be. There is continuity between capitalism and socialism. Not only are the means of production taken over from the one to the other, but the socialist superstructure takes over and develops to the fullest extent certain simple laws or rules which are necessary for the continuance of any society. Murder, for instance, is against the law in most societies. The law against murder in the Soviet Union continues a law of capitalist society, with the understanding that in socialist society the law is purified and applied to all men, not to the oppressed class only, as it supposedly is in capitalist society.

The discovery of specific laws of the development of socialism, however, has proved a disconcertingly difficult task for Soviet theoreticians. Thus far they have uncovered nothing that can be called a law in any strong sense of the term. What in fact is being used in governing and guiding society is not a set of laws but a set of norms and goals, which the party attempts to follow or reach with varying degrees of success and effort, for example, the planned and proportional character of economic development, the absense of antagonistic classes, brotherly collaboration and mutual help, and so on. It is difficult to determine clearly the means by which the society is to reach these goals. Invariably articles on scientific socialism list not laws but norms, and they call increasingly for specific sociological, psychological, or economic research and experimentation, which will hopefully reveal efficient ways of reaching the desired end of communism. Communism, the Soviet theoreticians now insist, must be *built*. It will not just happen. And experimentation is increasingly emphasized, though the experimentation allowed is contained within certain limits and must be geared toward the common goal of communism.

Libermanism is probably the best known of the recent Soviet experiments of this sort. Central planning, Marxist theory held, was to enable man to control the economy instead of being controlled by it; it was to render the economy rational, instead of letting individual greed or desires govern the economy at the expense of the over-all social welfare. But the task of completely controlling the economy from above proved highly complicated and resulted in many inefficiencies, poor quality goods that consumers did not need or want, and other difficulties. In the 1950's economists began asking for reforms, and in 1962 Yevsei Liberman, a professor of economics from Kharkov, published in *Pravda* an article calling for less direct administrative control of enterprises, leaving some decisions up to the local manager, and for the use of profit as the measure of the efficiency of an enterprise and as a source of material incentives for members of the enterprise. The proposals were not original with Liberman, but became associated with his name. They and other similar reforms were eventually tried on an experimental basis. On January 3, 1967, L. I. Brezhnev, Secretary-General of the CPSU Central Committee, said: "In 1966 about 700 industrial enterprises were operating according to the new system regarding economic reform. It is a vanguard in the realization of the economic reform. And the results of the work of these enterprises showed that the path had been paved correctly and that the main forces of our industry can also advance along it." [7] The economic reforms proposed and being cautiously implemented are not based on any supposed laws of socialist development, though they are geared toward such development. They represent a controlled experiment within the framework of building communism and not a denial or abandonment of this goal.

Just as the party still maintains strict control on economic experimentation it also controls sociological and psychological experimentation, and censorship still prevails over philosophical writings, literature, and the arts. The intellectuals have been attempting to escape political censorship, and in the past several years party policy has varied, now allowing more freedom, now tightening the reins. But the ending of official censorship will not guarantee complete freedom in the line of literature. For the publishing houses are government owned and controlled, and censorship by a party official will simply be replaced by the censorship of the publishing houses.

That values or norms and not specific laws of socialism are the present guides of Soviet society has not been generally admitted by Soviet ideologists, but the more candid of the new Soviet Marxists have acknowledged that values play an active role in the historical process, that man's free activity is determined by his ends and values, and that the historical development of socialism cannot be understood without understanding its ends and values.

Value Theory and Social Theory

The "social justice" of the Soviet economic system, though frequently ignored by Western analysts, is as sacred to Soviet economists as the sovereignty of "consumer choice" is to Western economists. The principle of "from each according to his ability, to each according to his need" is as normative a principle as the utilitarian one of "the greatest happiness for the greatest number." Yet neither these nor a host of other value judgments and norms widely used in organizing Soviet society were clearly grounded or explicated either by Marx or his successors. Until recently a general theory of value had been conspicuously lacking from Marxism-Leninism.

How can we explain the absence of a general value theory until now? How are we to account for its present emergence?

The most obvious reason why no general value theory developed earlier in Soviet philosophy is that none was presented by Marx and Lenin. According to Marx, there was no need for criticizing existing theories of value—with the exception of theories of economic value—or for developing a general theory of value. Ethical, cultural, and in general spiritual values were to change as the base changed; so Marx's main concern was with the base. He himself did not avoid making value judgments and his own normative claims were superimposed, interwoven, and confused with his descriptions. The new, progressive, proletarian values which he championed were supposedly the result of changing conditions and were thus factual reflections of a future reality which had already begun to develop.

This was Marx's position. Challenges to it were refuted by Lenin. From 1930 to 1947 philosophy was dominated by Stalin; and since the foundations of Marxism-Leninism were held sacred and were not to be tampered with, the failure of a value theory to develop during that period is understandable.

The recent change with respect to a general theory of value indicates both a development in Soviet philosophical thought and a revision of classical Marxist doctrine. The credit goes initially to Stalin. In opening up philosophical discussion in 1947 and in 1950 he emphasized the active role of the superstructure in Soviet society.[8] Following his death, the beginning of systematic philosophical analysis of the fundamental concepts of Marxism led to recognition of the need for a general Marxist theory of value. The revival of interest in the early, humanistic works of Marx by Georg Lukács and Western scholars further forced Soviet philosophers to consider questions of value if only to defend Marxism-Leninism against an unpalatable existentialist revisionism.

But these factors are secondary and came to bear only because of the needs of the party in blueprinting the development of Soviet society. It became clear to Stalin and to his successors that the values held by the masses had not changed automatically as a result of changes in economic relations. If changes in the base did not produce new men with a new, communist set of values, then these values had to be introduced directly, inculcated by education, propaganda, and the like. Since the laws of socialist development were based on a communist value system, the laws would not operate effectively unless the values were held by the mass of Soviet citizens. Dedication to the ends of a socialist and communist society had to replace the rule of force if the new, classless society was to emerge.

Just what the new theory of value consists of will become clearer in later chapters of this book. But it should already be clear that the new laws of socialist development which are now emerging are radically different from the iron laws of political economy presented by Marx in *Capital*.

The Yugoslav Variant

While the Soviets have been revising Marx's laws of social development implicitly, keeping the form while changing the content, the Yugoslav Marxists have been making bold and open innovations in the theory of socialism. Yugoslavia's split with Stalin and Stalinism in 1948 cleared the way for the search for alternatives; the availability of Western literature brought new perspectives; and a new approach arose. In the name of Marx, Stalin and Stalinism were criticized. In the name of Marx, Lenin was criticized; and there have even been times when in the name of Marx, Marx has been criticized.

In the other countries of Eastern Europe, the Soviet position with respect to socialism and the development of the laws of history represents the dominant line. Isolated Polish and Hungarian critics exist, but they are the outsiders. In 1966 Leszek Kolakowski, an outspoken philosopher and Polish revisionist, was expelled from the Communist Party for criticizing the way the party is governing Poland. The year before that two less widely known figures, Karol Modzelewski and Jacek Korun were sentenced to prison for circulating papers critical of conditions in Poland. Adam Schaff, a leading Polish Marxist, lost some of his power and prestige as a result of his book *Marxism and the Individual* in which he claims that alienation still exists in Poland and that socialism is not fulfilling the humanistic aspects of Marx's vision. The question of the presence of alienation within socialism was also raised in Hungary and the Soviet Union. But only in Yugoslavia has the criticism of existing conditions led to important changes.

In Yugoslavia, especially since 1960, a loosely organized group who consider themselves "creative Marxists" and who publish a journal called *Praxis* have been the strongest voice in philosophy and social theory. They do not hold political power, though they do influence social changes. Not all Yugoslav Marxists agree with them; and within the group itself there are men with Leninist leanings and others who ignore Lenin in favor of the humanism of early Marx. The influence of the group extends into other countries of Eastern Europe, and some of the more liberal thinkers from these countries have published in the journal. Though the group has more freedom of criticism and originality than any other group in Eastern Europe, there are limits beyond which it too is not allowed to go. Mihajlo Mihajlov and Djilas are sufficient reminders that complete freedom of criticism is not allowed. While differences and alternate suggestions are tolerated, any attempt to organize political opposition or introduce a multiparty system are still anathema.

The Yugoslav literature contains much less talk about the laws of history than is found among the Soviet writers. The tendency—just starting in the Soviet Union—to reinterpret the laws of history as trends, to water down claims of inevitability, and to emphasize values and ends as the proper guides in the development of society, has developed and is flourishing in Yugoslavia. Talk of the "inevitability of communism" has been replaced by claims of its "objective possibility." This means that while capitalism provides the basis in wealth and goods necessary to achieve communism, and while the necessary social transformations can be achieved, there is no guarantee that they will be.

There are four aspects of the "creative Marxist" position on socialism and social development which differ significantly from the Soviet model: 1) its rejection of the doctrine of *partiinost'*; 2) its doctrine of many roads to socialism; 3) its criticism of Soviet socialism; and 4) its development of the doctrine of socialist self-management. Each of these requires a closer examination.

1) The doctrine of *partiinost'* is a Leninist addition to Marxism, which has been continued down to the present. According to Lenin the party represents the working masses; it is the vanguard of the proletariat and as such is the most progressive element of mankind. Its function is to lead and guide the development of mankind to socialism and then to communism. It has a ruling role in society. It preserves, guards, and develops Marxist doctrine, and armed with this doctrine enjoys a privileged role in society's development.

Under Stalin the party—and especially its leader—came to be regarded as omnicompetent. The doctrine of *partiinost'* or partisanship or party-mindedness grew into the claim that the party was the last word and arbiter in all realms of knowledge and social life. The party acted as official judge and censor of art, literature, philosophy, science, and all other domains. Stalin was the ultimate authority in the linguistics controversy; the party's defense of Lysenko made his views the dominant views in biology in the Soviet Union for a long period despite the scientific evidence against them; the party's negative reaction to relativity and quantum mechanics, cybernetics and symbolic logic kept them for a long time from being accepted and developed in the Soviet Union. The party's line on socialist realism dictated what was acceptable and what was not in art.

The first part of the doctrine of *partiinost'* to be challenged in Yugoslavia and later in most of the other satellite countries was the omnicompetence of the Communist Party of the Soviet Union. As long as there was only one socialist country there was in fact only one successful communist party. With the rise of several socialist countries and the simultaneous rise of national communist parties ruling different countries, the question of which communist party was the spokesman for the masses arose. When Yugoslavia separated itself from Stalin in 1948, the Yugoslav Communist Party assumed for itself the leadership of at least the Yugoslavs. After 1956 other countries of Eastern Europe, as well as China, no longer recognized the hegemony of the Communist Party of the Soviet Union—at least not in many questions of their own internal affairs. The doctrine of *partiinost'* was undermined because there were many centers of power and many communist parties. The doctrine was wedded to political power and it survived or not on a national level as the possessors of that power chose. In the Soviet Union it has remained. In Poland and Hungary it has been diluted. In Yugoslavia the doctrine of the party's omnicompetence has given way to that of its leadership in politics and economics, though where politics and economics end is still debated.

Yugoslav philosophy, its practitioners claim, is no longer the handmaiden of politics. Philosophy and politics are related. But each has its own sphere. And philosophers make the whole world, including politics, the object of their criticism. In criticizing the doctrine of *partiinost'* Gajo Petrović claims "Yugoslav Marxists have now overcome the Stalinistic dogmas about philosophy as a servant of politics and about party as the supreme judge in philosophic disputes . . ."[9] Andrija Krešić goes a step further, criticizing the party's claim to act in the name of the proletariat, and pointing out that having the party in power is not the same as having the class in power and that only the latter is the Marxist aim.[10]

2) The Soviet Union built its own road to socialism. It had no predecessors and no specific guide. It was not the path Marx had vaguely foreseen; for Russia at the time of the revolution was not one of the advanced industrial powers, but was still largely a rural country with a peasant economy. Forced industrialization, the liquidation of the class of kulaks and political opponents of any form, the collectivization of agriculture, and the use of terror were all part of the Soviet transition to socialism. Was the Soviet way the only way?

Yugoslavia claimed not, and chose to go its own way, pave its own road. That there are several roads to socialism, that each country must go at its own pace, and that different ways may be possible is now a doctrine of the Soviet as well as other Marxisms. In the Soviet view, however, the Soviet Union remains the prime example of a socialist country, for it is furthest along the road, and has already entered the stage of building communism. This claim is explicitly rejected by many Yugoslav Marxists, and leads directly to their critique of Soviet socialism.

3) It is commonplace for non-Marxist critics to criticize the Soviet Union and its social system. It is unheard of for Soviet Marxists to do so, except if they are deploring the personality cult and its abuses. The new Marxists of Yugoslavia hold the Soviet Union—and to a lesser extent Yugoslavia—fair game.

The Yugoslav critics of Soviet socialism are of two kinds. The less radical and violent recognize the Bolshevik Revolution as Marxist, and the development of socialism in the Soviet Union as significant and progressive. Their complaint is that especially in recent years the Soviet Union has had the material base to progress faster and more directly toward communism. Instead of doing so it has tended to become bureaucratic, its leaders have tended to form a ruling class unwilling to give up its power, and the impetus towards communism has been checked.

The more radical critics go much further and hold at least implicitly that the revolution has been betrayed. The Marxist revolution was to be a revolution of the working class by the working class to achieve their freedom and realize their aims and ends. Instead, in Russia there was a revolution by a party which, while pretending to speak in the name of the workers, proclaimed its own principles and imposed them on the workers, and which rules the workers, instead of letting them rule themselves. While "state capitalism" is the term often used by Western critics to describe this result, the Yugoslavs use the term "statism." S. Stojanović defines "statism" as "a system based on state ownership of the means of production and state control over production and other social activities. The state apparatus represents a new ruling class. As the collective owner of the means of production it employs labor and exploits it. The personal share of a member of the ruling class in the distribution of the surplus value is in direct proportion to his position in the state hierarchy."[11] Its paradigms, he claims, are Stalinism and Maoism. But the criticism applies wherever it fits.

This Marxist criticism of existing types of socialism is not made from some external point of reference but on the basis of the works of Marx himself. The working class does not control production and has no voice in the distribution of surplus value; the nationalization of land turned the peasant into a part of the exploited proletariat; and a new exploitive class has seized political and economic power to achieve what are their own but not necessarily the people's aims. The critique stems from the lack of humanism evident in the historical development of the Soviet Union, as opposed to the humanism which permeates Marx's early works. Gajo Petrović states: "One of the basic achievements of our postwar philosophical development is the discovery that man, who was excluded from the Stalinistic version of Marxist philosophy as an abstraction, is in the center of authentic Marx's philosophic thought."[12]

At the heart of the matter is the role of the state in socialist development. In classical Marxism the state was seen as an instrument of oppression, used by the ruling class to protect their interests and keep the ruled subservient. With the proletarian revolution the state was to wither away. While both the Soviet and the Yugoslav Marxists agree that the state will wither, the Soviet view is that it will only wither with the achievement of full-scale communism. Until then it is not only necessary but must be strengthened. The 1961 Program of the CPSU stated further "The period of full-scale communist construction is characterized by a further *enhancement of the role and importance of the Communist Party* as the leading and guiding force of Soviet society."[13] By contrast the Yugoslav Marxists claim that there should not simply be an *ultimate* transfer of power from the state to the people but that this should take place as soon as possible; that true socialism is not characterized by rule by a party but by self-rule of the workers; and that the state withers not by first being strengthened but by being weakened.

4) The Yugoslav Marxist alternative to statism is "self-management socialism." In the Marxist critical vein they insist that every moment of history must be evaluated in terms of Marxist hu-

manism and man's freedom. Consequently no social system is immune from criticism and every stage in the development of socialism must be evaluated. The ideal of communism is not something fixed and determined either by Marx or by the communist party of any country. It is a condition of society in which the aims of all men, expressed by them and not by their supposed or self-appointed spokesman, are achieved. The "creative Marxists" seem convinced that there is some set of norms or goals which all men in their society wish to implement or achieve, that these are social, and that they can only be achieved by communal effort. But they do not spell out these goals in detail. Their concern moreover is not only with the standard of living. The poverty of capitalism consists not in its low standard of living but in its alienation and enslavement of the workers, and these are to be avoided.

According to Mihailo Marković, democratic or self-management socialism is the negation of state socialism (or statism) and bureaucracy. It requires "a reasonable number of rational, socialized, and human persons who understand the major aim of the social process, persons who are themselves alive to the relative interlinking of personal, group, and general interests and who base their activities on ideals of general human significance." [14] While an undeveloped rural society does not have such people, and they must be trained by a revolutionary elite, the elite in turn must turn over the reins once they are produced. Marković contends that the Soviet leaders refuse to make the change, that China does not have the prerequisites, but that Yugoslavia is moving in the proper direction.

For Marković self-management avoids the centralism-decentralization dispute by forming both central and lower level organs of self-management.

Exactly how self-management is to be implemented remains in part unanswered. In the economic sphere decision-making has been largely turned over to the factories. Unlike the Soviet experiments, the Yugoslavs are calling for the workers to make decisions jointly, for factory cooperatives to run the factories, and for all to share in the profits. The party is being reorganized and separated from the government, and its governing role is being reduced. The party is "to lead and influence but not to control." [15] Exactly how the factories would operate and gauge their proper limits of profit, how the unsuccessful would be cared for or helped, and how exploitation of others by the cooperatives would be prevented remain as yet unsettled. But the Yugoslavs are backing theory with practice and are pursuing a new, and they claim, authentically Marxist, though not necessarily Leninist and certainly not Stalinist, approach. Whether the party or the state will wither away remains, of course, to be seen. But the thought of their doing so fills the "creative Marxists"—unlike their Soviet or East European counterparts—not with fear but with anticipation.

These new Marxists do not claim to have uncovered the laws of the development of self-management socialism, though they hope to reach it by trial and error, if by no other way. They, like more conservative new Marxists, are convinced that the wave of the future is not capitalism. But it is clear to them that statism is not enough. They see capitalism as moving closer and closer to statism and the centralism and bureaucracy it involves.

One cry of the new Marxists is for freedom and humanism, for a man-centered society. The meaning of man in the new Marxism therefore deserves careful consideration.

3

The Marxist Vision of Man

■ Every politics, ethics, or social theory has implicit in it a certain view of man. Marxism is no exception. Marx's writings, though they contain no systematic discussion of man, contain many statements about what he has been, what he is, and what he can become.

In 1962, V. P. Tugarinov, a Soviet Professor of Philosophy at the University of Leningrad, noted that the problem of the person was just beginning to be raised in Marxism-Leninism.[1] It still has not progressed very far. But it has developed sufficiently for us to piece together the Soviet view of man—a view which also serves as something of a blueprint for the development of the new Soviet man. Communist society requires "new men" to people it if it is to work; and if these are not produced spontaneously by the changing economic base of society, then they must be produced by other means: by education, propaganda, the force of public opinion, by laws and social pressures, and by any other means possible.

Neither Marx nor most contemporary Marxists bother to distinguish between the descriptive and evaluative use of "man," between references to present-day man and to man-of-the-future, or between men considered as individual beings and men considered collectively. The term "man" is usually used indiscriminately to cover all of these. Since it is only by keeping straight the various meanings and uses that we can achieve clarity about their views, I shall make the appropriate distinctions in the discussion that follows.

As with so much of the new Marxism, the raw material for this view of man is found primarily in the early writings of Marx. The development of recent Soviet interest in this area has a threefold source. It stems partly from pressures arising from Western, especially existentialist, interpretations of these writings. It reflects the necessity for consciously molding the "new man" who has not developed spontaneously in the Soviet Union. And it serves as grist for the Soviet propaganda mill. As the Soviet philosopher L. V. Nikolaeva put it: "The question of the person and his freedom in the present day stands at the center of the ideological struggle." [2] The problems of the individual, which had long been submerged in the problems of the class in Marxist writings, are now beginning to rise to the surface.

Man as Changing and Changeable

Three characteristics stand out in the Soviet view of man. He is changing and changeable; he is changed by his work; and he is what he is only collectively or in society.

The Soviet approach to man is historical. There is no common quality or nature which each individual man in the past, present, and future has or shares. The search for the abstract essence of man is thus a futile one. Reason is not the distinguishing character of man, despite Aristotle's famous dictum that man is a rational animal. For reason and consciousness, like speech, arise from need and intercourse with other men. Reason is not something which man received full-blown as a gift from the gods. Consciousness developed as need developed. Man from his early origins to the present and on into the future changes as his needs change. The historical development of man must be seen as being *historical* and as *development*. Man can be said to be distinguished from other animals by the fact that he produces his means of subsistence, by the fact that he changes the conditions of his production, by the fact that he has consciousness and uses speech, or by any number of other characteristics. All of these assertions are to some extent true. But they take on meaning and content only when seen in their historical development. Consciousness, like man, is historical and develops. It is not an eternal, finished characteristic of man, but a social product; and so it has a status similar to the concept "man." Little is gained therefore by defining "man" in terms of "consciousness."

In the Marxist-Leninist view the full meaning of man can be found only by summing up everything that man has been and will be. But such a fully "concrete universal" is, of course, not available to us, since man is not finished. At our present stage of development we can at best see what man has been, and what he may become, and we can attempt to give adequate expression to this by describing man's historical development. According to the Marxists the mistake of many previous views of man is that they have taken the men of their times as the paradigm for man in general. They have generalized the citizens of the Greek city-state, or the bourgeoisie of Western Europe in the eighteenth century into some eternal, unchanging concept of man.

According to the Marxist view, man is a natural being, a part of nature, who evolved biologically from the ape. But biological evolution is neither the whole story, nor indeed the most significant part of man's evolution. For especially in the last phase of the formation of man, after his body had acquired its present basic structure, social factors came into play even more than biological ones. What Marx and Engels have added to the general notion of man's evolution is that it is *work* which separates man from the ape. It is by work that man creates himself, and it is by work that he will continue to change and evolve. It is by his labor, by acting on the external world and changing it, that he changes his own nature. Labor, Engels tells us and contemporary Soviet philosophers repeat, created man himself.[3] Together with labor came the need for and the gradual development of speech and of consciousness, and eventually, with the appearance of "fully fledged man" came society. It is by work that man evolved, but it is only in society that he actually became man. Man appears only with society. Gradual changes led man from his higher ape ancestors. Through his work he became a being qualitatively different from the apes, a social being who through the recognition of nature's laws is able to apply them and gain mastery over nature.

Marx and Engels tell us, "as individuals express their life, so they are. What they are, therefore, coincides with their production: both with *what* they produce and with *how* they produce. The nature of individuals thus depends on the material conditions determining their production."[4] The way men produce the means of their subsistence is the way they express their lives. But this is not all that man is, for built on their production is the social superstructure of society, their institutions, laws, art, culture, religion, philosophy.

The search for the meaning of "man" is therefore to be found not in the analysis of any individual considered in isolation from his fellow men and society. Rather it is to be sought primarily in the material conditions which make men what they are. The Soviet view of man is based on Marx's sixth Thesis on Feuerbach, which is almost invariably quoted in Soviet discussions of this topic: "Feuerbach resolves the essence of religion in the essence of *man*. But the essence of man is no abstraction inherent in each separate individual. In its reality it is the *ensemble* of social relations."

As the ensemble of social relations changes, so the essence of man changes. Insofar as the universal term "man" has content, it stands for the sum of all individual men; and insofar as the phrase "essence of man" has content, it stands for the sum of all social relations. Any individual man is the product of his epoch: his thoughts, feelings, and conduct are determined by the ensemble of social relations, which includes his national, family, political, legal, ideological and other relations, though basic to them all are the economic relations or relations of production, which correspond to a definite stage of development of material productive forces. Neanderthal man is not the same as the twentieth-century German or Russian because his means of production and the society in which he lives, which is based upon them, are different. Economic conditions establish limits to the variety of individuals in any historical epoch, and what is bound by these limits has often been taken by philosophers to be the essence of man. But at best these limits define the essence of the men of that particular epoch.

Work is the means by which man distinguished himself from other animals. An individual consequently expresses himself in a characteristically human way only when he works, and only to the extent that he is a worker. Moreover, just as man has made himself what he is by his labor, so it is by his labor that man will change himself. It is by labor that men will change the material conditions of their production, and these will bring about corresponding changes in man's social relations, and so in man himself. The Marxist view therefore contains both a technique for describing men in different stages of historical development and a key to changing them.

There is one further aspect of the Soviet view of man which is central to Soviet theory and actions. Man is for the Marxists a social being, and even more a collective being. Aristotle and others, of course, observed that man was a social being long before Marx. But in the hands of Marx and of his Marxist-Leninist followers this takes on a new meaning and significance. Since the essence of man is the ensemble of his social relations three things follow.

1) The individual is defined not in terms of what he is in himself, taken as an individual, but rather in terms of his relations to others. For apart from them he has no human essence; he is said to be a man, and different from animals, only because he has these relations. Man is an object related to other objects in a certain, special, social manner, and an individual is a man only when so related.

2) It follows from this that human reality is in a sense derivative. For man receives his nature only from society, into which he is born. Society produced *man as man,* though society is produced by man. For Soviet Marxists man and society are interrelated, neither being primary either in time or ontologically. But it should be noted here that it is *men* and society that are interrelated and that any given *individual* man is born into an already established society. Society is thus anterior to present-day individuals. Primacy devolves on society rather

than on an individual wherever there is a conflict of interests. For the individual is only a part of the whole and consequently subordinate to it.

3) Though according to this theory man is the maker of man this is not to be understood in an existentialist fashion. For individual men do not make themselves; rather men collectively make themselves. An individual man receives his essence from the social relations of his society and these were formed not by any man in isolation or alone, but by the men of that society taken together. Moreover what the men of a society can achieve, even together, is not the result of their arbitrary whim or fiat. Each generation inherits its productive forces and forms of social intercourse and so inherits its essence, which it can at best modify to some extent. Man makes himself but he does so only collectively and only to the extent that he changes the material conditions of the life of his society.

Man and Culture

The Soviet view of man which we have thus far outlined is man seen objectively, as an object of nature related to the rest of nature. This view of man is descriptive and non-evaluative. Each individual, because he lives in society, is socially related to other men and so is himself a man. Though men from epoch to epoch or from class to class differ in their social relations, and so differ in their essence, the view of man we have seen seems to be sufficiently neutral so that men in each epoch and class can with equal justification be called men. As far as we have gone, then, "man" is in no sense an honorific but is merely a descriptive term. It is neither good nor bad to be a man, and so there is no reason for excluding any individual from the class of men. Nor would it make any sense to speak of entities of any epoch being more or less human than those of any other epoch.

However, the Marxist-Leninist view of man superimposes upon this neutral description of man valuational aspects or uses of the term "man." The first of these arises from a consideration of the subjective or personal side of man; the second from an ideal image of what man can and will become, in terms of which earlier states of man are seen as inferior to his later development.

The Soviet view of man does not deny his subjective, inner, or so-called spiritual life. But it must be correctly understood. For man's inner world or his spiritual or cultural life—which includes all his ideas, feelings, representations, values, and goods distinct from material life—is not a separate, independent world unto itself. Rather it is derivative and based upon the objective world, of which it is a reflection. Mind or consciousness, according to Marxism-Leninism, is the highest product of matter, but it is derivative and not original; it is a quality or function of matter. Through consciousness man can bring into himself in a reflective manner what exists objectively outside of himself. His cultural world is a reflection of the material world and is based upon it. The richness of a person's inner life can vary and is always limited by the richness of the society in which he lives, its social relations, and its existing culture. An individual's spiritual richness is thus a function both of the cultural richness of his society and of his reflection or appropriation of this richness. It includes the development of his talents in physical and mental work through education and practice, the development of his feelings, and the development of his inner life by mastering the achievements of human culture.

In the perspective of his internal, subjective, spiritual development man can be considered in terms of his "person" or "personality." (There is only one word, *lichnost'* in Russian and it has both meanings.) In the Soviet view not every man is necessarily a person, and in history certainly not every man has been so considered. A slave, for example, was not considered a person by the slaveholder. Personality is a social phenomenon; it, like man, is a product of society. According to V. P. Tugarinov, Marxism-Leninism does not identify "man" and "personality." Personality is a property of man—better yet, of some men—and the judgment of who is considered a person depends on the society in which people live.[5]

The Soviet notion of personality admits of degrees. Individuals may be more or less fully developed persons. Historically, the development of the term "person," according to Marxism-Leninism, is closely related to the development of the term "man" and the two have often been interchanged. In primitive society man in a tribal community identified himself with his tribe or clan and had no consciousness of himself as an individual. As society developed, classes arose. With the rise of classes there arose individual self-consciousness on the part of the exploiting minority who stood above the masses. Even the Greeks who developed a great culture considered most men as slaves; they were not persons, but things to be bought and sold and used as one wished. Yet the Greek citizen had the opportunity for all-round development of his personality to a fuller degree than the man of bourgeois society, who is impeded in his development by the existing division of labor. In bourgeois society personality becomes a function of capital, of money and possessions. According to Marxism-Leninism it is only under communism that each man will be recognized as a person and achieve his full all-round development.

"Person" is thus an honorific. Personality is both something which can be achieved and which it is morally good to achieve. Since personality is formed and recognized by society, societies can be judged moral or immoral, better or worse, depending on whether they foster or hinder the development of personality.

This development consists in the development of self-consciousness, of consciousness of one's connections with others, and of culture, inclinations, and taste.[6] Personality is not developed by individual effort alone but only through mutual help and education. Richness of personality presupposes an existing richness of society, cultural and other, which can be reflected. The perfection of man consists in the fullest development of his personality. This in turn requires the perfection and development of society. Experience and education heighten the value of individual life for oneself and for society; the more an individual mirrors reality the more value he possesses. But his value is always derived from society and subordinate to it.

Man is not a disembodied spirit unfettered by natural laws. Just as man's spiritual life is a reflection of his material life, he acts most effectively when he directs his actions in accordance with known laws of nature. His ability to act with knowledge of laws is not a property of spirit but of human activity. Man will be free to develop himself, therefore, only when: 1) he correctly reflects or knows the laws governing reality; and 2) he is not impeded from engaging in labor in keeping with his inclinations. Man often feels his potentiality cramped and he desires to expand and express himself. Only when he has the opportunity and ability to do so can he be said to be free to develop and assert himself as a personality. According to Marxism-Leninism the requisite knowledge is achieved primarily through mastering the "creative ideas of Marxism-Leninism."[7] The necessary conditions can be found only in a society in which there is no exploitation and in which personal and social aims coincide, i.e., in a communist society. Thus for Marxism-Leninism man can fully realize himself as a person and achieve maximum value only under communism.

The Progressive Development of Man

If we now join the descriptive or objective view of man and the evaluative or subjective view of him as a person, we can complete the Marxist-Leninist view of man. The two elements are fused for the most part in the writings of Marx and in those of the Soviet philosophers writing on man. Based on the relation of these two elements Marxism-Leninism develops an ideal view of man in terms of which men of different societies can be judged. The historical development of man consists of his emergence from primitive society, through class society, to his complete development in communist society.

According to Marx, when man began to emerge from primitive society he formed a class society based on private property and the division of labor. The result was a discrepancy between the essence and the existence of man or between his objective and subjective facets. The essence of man is collective, something that he makes together with other men and which they share. But in his individual existence in a class

society man found himself separated from and opposed to
other men. The essence of man includes all human culture
and all social relations. But the individual separated from
others could realize and reflect only a microscopic part of
his essence. Man created man; but measured against his
essence the individual in class societies was found poor. As
a result of the division of labor individual men became "partial men" or truncated persons who made and possessed only
a fragment of human culture because the rest belonged to
others.

In a class society, according to Marxism-Leninism, the condition of "war of all against all" exists, and man is separated,
opposed to other men, and so fragmented in his existence.
The product of his labor, the means by which he expresses
himself, is appropriated by another. His labor, his productive
activity, is the means by which he should express himself;
but he is forced to sell this to another, to the capitalist; and
so labor becomes not a way of life but a means of keeping
himself alive by selling himself. Each seeks to possess what
he can and so does not share. What should be common is
private; what should unite men—their labor and what they
produce—divides them. The division of society is reflected in
the division of man, whose essence becomes fragmented, whose
existence becomes partial, whose development is constrained,
and whose personality—at least in the case of the oppressed,
exploited masses—atrophies. At best in a class society we can
speak of "class men" who reflect their class.

In the Soviet view man can overcome his separation from
himself only when the causes of division, namely private
property and the division of labor, are abolished. Only when
man is not separated from other men and when he can express himself in his labor, can the split between man's essence
and existence, between his subjective and objective facets,
be overcome. Only by abolishing classes can man emerge
from class-man to man as such, fully reflecting the totality
of his essence. Such is the ideal of man and it can be realized,
supposedly, only when society is organized in a communistic
manner. Only then will man be fully man and will each man

be a person, free to engage in the all-round development of his personality and in the unfolding of all his talents and abilities. The fact that man is presently only partial and truncated is not a cause for pessimism but for optimism. For man is still to be made, the best is yet to come, and man's fullness will be realized when communism, the wave of the future, is finally realized.

As a result of this view several consequences are drawn by Soviet Marxists. 1) Not only are men of capitalist society partial, truncated men, cut off from the full enjoyment of the collective essence of capitalist society, but since this essence falls short of the ideal, men who acquiesce in it are not what they can and should become. Consequently these men, as a class, are immoral. 2) Because man makes himself by his labor, work assumes moral value in Soviet society. Individuals who do not work are called parasites, considered immoral and subject to legal prosecution. For in so acting they in a sense deny their humanity: though capable of doing so, they fail to express themselves humanly through their labor. 3) The "builders of communism," it is claimed, are builders not only of a new society founded on new productive relations, but they are also the builders of better men, of the "new men" who will people that society and who will reflect the unfragmented essence which results from an unfragmented society. The emphasis is not only on labor but on "conscientious labor for the good of society." The Soviet concept of a good man is thus one of a future-oriented, dynamic worker, struggling to produce a better society, and struggling against both the forces of nature and the bourgeois, capitalistic influences which he has inherited and which still surround him. Consequently both an individual's fulfillment and his happiness depend on his engaging in this struggle; it is in this struggle that he is to find the meaning of life. This is the image of man fostered and promulgated in the Soviet Union. 4) According to Marxism-Leninism the value of an individual is extrinsic and is either a product of his usefulness to society, or is derived from the fact that he reflects the value of society. At best he is a brick of the social building[8] and has the value of being part of a valuable whole. In himself and of himself, however, considered apart from society, he has no intrinsic value and can scarcely be called a man in any sense of the word. According to A. F. Shishkin, a prolific Soviet philosopher, whoever remains outside the struggle for communism is not yet conscious of his human dignity; whoever becomes an instrument of exploiters deprives himself of his dignity.[9] If the fullest blooming of man is possible only in future communist society, present-day man can achieve his greatest value only by engaging in socially valuable work which will lead to communism.

Man and the Party

According to the Soviet view, man is a natural, social, work-oriented being who develops collectively through history and will reach his fulfillment under communism. This view presents a model of what man should be. But how is he to be produced? The classical Marxist answer would be by work. The present Soviet answer adds other aspects of education which are necessary to offset the lag of social consciousness behind social being. Work is still basic and is itself considered a form of education. To it are added propaganda and education through all means including newspapers, literature, and art. If man is not yet formed, not yet full-grown, he is still immature, still being formed. And he is treated accordingly by the party, which has assumed the role of teacher of the worker and of all mankind. The result in the Soviet Union is paternalism.

The working masses are to be formed, trained, molded. The Soviet Marxist philosophical and party literature is full of articles on the role of labor in the education of the worker, on the necessity of inculcating the Marxist-Leninist world view, and on discussions of the most effective means to achieve this education. The role of the communist party as teacher as well as leader and the need to educate the masses is reiterated by each of the Party Congresses, and enlarged upon by Soviet Marxists.[10]

In the Soviet view an adult is not yet a fully formed man capable of choosing his own ends and assuming responsibility for his decisions. To speak of man as mature smacks of individualism. It neglects the collective essence of man and ignores the common end of all mankind, the achievement of communism. This, according to Soviet Marxists, is the only proper end of man and the one which all men must be taught. To help the individual learn this, to help him place common interests before his own and to teach him how to live and work in harmony with his fellow men, is one of the chief aims of the Soviet educational program.

Soviet paternalism involves not only education but other aspects of the parental function as well. The party seeks to protect its members against error, it tries to care for their needs as far as possible, given the Soviet Union's resources and competing demands; and when necessary, as a firm parent, it uses force to ensure compliance.

The role of teacher is assumed by the party because, as we have seen, it claims scientific knowledge of the social development of Soviet society, and because it claims that over-all social direction is a prerequisite of the successful attainment of communism. The members of the party, and its leaders, it is true, are not fully formed; for man can only be fully formed in a communist society, which has yet to be built. But since the party is the vanguard of presently existing mankind, the task of direction falls to it, if only by default.

The Soviet justification for communism has in recent years been put in terms of man. Communist education, it is claimed, has as its task the formation of a rational man. The ultimate goal of all the activities of the CPSU is said to be to make the life of man secure and to create conditions for the flowering of his creative powers and his abilities. A. F. Shishkin proclaims that man is the most valuable entity in the world.[11]

One difficulty with these and similar statements is the ambiguity in the use of the term "man." The ideal is to provide the opportunity for the full all-round development of each man in communist society; but communist society has not yet been realized. When "man" is said to be the most valuable entity, "man" means the fully developed man of the future. It also means man taken collectively, not individual men who, as parts of the whole, are always subordinate to it. The questions of subordination and of the opposition of the individual to the collective, are brushed aside, however, even by otherwise rather outspoken Soviet Marxists with the platitude that under communism individual and social interests will coincide. Until communism is reached, individual interests must give way to social interests and the individual must be taught to make his interests conform to society's. Present men must make sacrifices for future man.

One of the major shortcomings of the Soviet view of man, which has been mentioned by many non-Soviet Marxists, is its inadequate treatment of man's personal, subjective, individual life. In the Soviet view so far it has only derivative, secondary importance, and treatments of the life of individual men have been swallowed up in the consideration of man as a member of a class or group, of man as a collective, social being, and of the ideal of man as fully developed in communist society. Whether the new society will produce the new man is a crucial test of Soviet theory. But in the interim other new Marxists are attempting to fill the gap.

Marxism and the Individual

The need of Marxism to turn its attention to the concerns of the individual was brought to a head by the popularity of existentialism in some of the countries of Eastern Europe. In particular it was the attraction of Jean-Paul Sartre among young Polish literary and intellectual groups that moved Adam Schaff to turn his attention to the problems of a philosophy of man. The result has been in his case a number of articles and books. In *A Philosophy of Man,* a collection of his essays published in the United States in 1963, he sketches a Marxist philosophy of man and analyzes such topics as the meaning of life, freedom, responsibility, and happiness. But despite his turning to these problems his solutions remain within the structure of the materialist conception of history and he insists on the social understanding of the individual and on the social conditions for happiness. In a later book, *Marxism and the Individual*,[12] he takes a pragmatic approach to the individual and to a defense of his rights. He insists that man is the supreme being for man and acknowledges that in socialism this ideal has not yet been reached. He then goes on to a criticism of some aspects of socialism as fostering certain kinds of human alienation. But despite all this he does not actually add anything significant to the Soviet Marxist view of man. He sees, perhaps, that there are problems in the philosophy of man which Marxism has not answered; but he does not produce any answers. Even in his criticism of Polish socialism, his critique comes later than that of other Poles, and he has not gone as far as others, for instance Kolakowski, whose critique of Polish socialism and the inefficiencies of its leaders Schaff himself condemned.

If we turn to the Yugoslav Marxists we find at least an implicit criticism of the Soviet Marxist view of man. Its paternalistic aspect is especially distasteful to some. While Schaff, like the Soviet Marxists says, "the central problem—how to make people happy—will be of ever greater importance,"[13] Mihailo Marković speaks against the view of socialism as "a type of enforced happiness, in which the man who is making someone happy never stops speaking in the name of the man who is made happy. The notion of social self-management," he continues, "presupposes a fundamentally different conception of man."[14] In a society in which there is a high degree of material and spiritual culture in the masses, man will be sociable, rational, and creative. In this case "there is no reason to think that some self-appointed guardian of the general interest can be superior in relation to the total brain strength of the society whose interests these are."[15]

Svetozar Stojanović argues against a "collectivistic deformation of Marxism" claiming that the core of Marxism is the individual, not man in general. But the personalistic view of man which he claims is specific to Marx ("totalization, socialization, de-alienation, liberation, democratization, etc.") remains vague.[16] One thing, however, is clear for Stojanović, and that is that no ideal of man should ever be treated as if it could be achieved. Man's development never ends. Our view of him must therefore be left open; and presumably there will be no future time, in or out of communism, when man can be said to be complete.

The rejection of paternalism conforms to the Yugoslav notion of self-management; the reduced emphasis on collectivism allows more room in the present for free expression. This indicates how a view of man may be a reflection of specific social practices.

A thoroughgoing philosophical discussion of the person has yet to be developed in the new Marxism. But perhaps the most fascinating hint of what might be forthcoming comes from a Czech philosopher, Karel Kosík,[17] some of whose works have been translated into several languages. He sees that Marxism must handle those problems which have been taken up by the existentialists in their protest against dehumanization; but he rejects both Marxist and other attempts to split man into inwardness and outwardness, subjectivity and objectivity, and to deal with abstractions instead of with real men. His claim is that the individual does not have priority over the collective, nor should the collective subjugate individual interests to its own ends. For both approaches deprive the individual of his responsibility.

Kosík accepts the Marxist notion that man is both a product of history and a maker of history. The individual can integrate into his life what is generally human, and what has been developed historically by men before him. But these qualities must be assimilated and totalized, reproduced and revived by a particular human individual for them to have meaning and value. What it means to be human has developed historically; but the living out of human life must always be done individually. Individuals who accept this responsibility become autonomous. They conform neither positively nor negatively, they are neither subsumed by the collective nor do they negate or oppose it. What this approach has that the Soviet view lacks is a means of reconciling man as a collective being and man as an individual person, allowing each to have value while showing where the value of each lies.

It also does not reject present men as incomplete or unfinished, while admitting that in some ways they may not have reached the integration or totalization that might be achieved in the future. It does not necessarily justify present sacrifice in the name of a mythical future, and it leaves room for value and principles in the present as well as in the future. The notion of autonomy also militates against Soviet paternalism and allows for the existence of mature, responsible adults at each stage of man's development.

What more will be forthcoming from the new Marxists in their approach to man remains to be seen. The question of value, both in general and with reference to individuals remains to be worked out, as does a theory of rights, other than the simple positivism which states that the individual has whatever rights the state wishes to bestow upon him, and that what the state gives, the state can also take away.

The meaning and status of mind is also an unresolved area in the Marxist view of man. Supposedly mind is the highest product of matter, though not reducible to it. Precisely what this means, how mind has come to evolve, and what its status and function are have yet to be clarified. Some Marxists are turning to the view that at every level of reality matter has something analagous to the mind's power to reflect reality outside of it; and that this emerges clearly only in man because of his highly complex structure. The theory is still, however, in an embryonic stage.

In the realm of psychology Soviet psychologists have relied heavily on Pavlov. Makarenko's ideas concerning the influence of the group on the individual have been developed with respect to education and social pressures. But social psychology has not progressed very far in the Soviet Union as yet, and individual psychology has not turned its attention to the individual *qua* individual sufficiently to contribute anything to the Marxist view of man. Sex, love, hate, the desire for power or suicide, and other tendencies claimed as basic to man by some Western psychologists play no important part in the Marxist view of man. Transcendence, mystery, and the unknown are precluded. Work is what is central and the fact that man can be changed. He is basically neither good nor bad but the product of his society.

Marxist emphasis has historically been on classes and the masses as the makers of history. The place and role of the individual has been a stumbling block, and what was said of individuals was based on deductions from the materialist theory of history. Men were what they were and their actions were determined ultimately by their economic position, though individual idiosyncrasies were allowed for. Individual actions could not be predicted or completely explained; but these after all did not determine history. Present-day Marxists are now looking closer at the individual, who seems to slip out of the net of classical Marxism. And if detailed explanations of and solutions to the problems of men as individuals and personalities are not yet available, most of the new Marxists at least defend future man in general terms and champion socialist humanism. This humanism forms part of the next topic we shall have to investigate.

4

Humanism, Alienation, and Existentialism

■ The jump from man to humanism is a short one and one made more and more frequently in contemporary Marxist theory. Marxism has always been humanistic in some sense. Marx claimed that communism was a humanism, and he was centrally concerned with man, his plight, and the improvement of his conditions. But though the claim of humanism has been part of Marxist theory from the start, for many years it was not given much prominence and received lip-service rather than serious discussion or implementation. Throughout the Stalinist period humanism in the Soviet Union remained a theme played in a minor key. In more recent years it has been played louder and longer by the new Marxists of the Soviet Union and Eastern Europe. Characteristically the Soviet tune is the simplest and in many ways the harshest. Variations and innuendos are developed by the same East European philosophers who are interested in the question of man and orchestrated into a much more interested presentation.

Soviet Marxist humanism is equivalent to communism. In keeping with the Soviet concept of man, communist humanism is thoroughly collectivist. Its central aim is the de-alienation of society. And it is unequivocally atheistic.

The Meaning of Communism

A future state of society, communism has never been very fully defined. For Marx and Engels, as well as for Lenin, it was a condition too far distant to be seen distinctly. Marx, as we have seen, described it mostly in contrast to bourgeois society. The fullest statement we have comes from Part Two of the 1961 Program of the Communist Party of the Soviet Union—a document associated with Khrushchev and now not frequently quoted:

> Communism is a classless social system with one form of public ownership of the means of production and full social equality of all members of society; under it, the all-round development of people will be accompanied by the growth of productive forces through continuous progress in science and technology; all the springs of cooperative wealth will flow more abundantly, and the great principle "From each according to his ability, to each according to his needs" will be implemented. Communism is a highly organized society of free, socially conscious working people in which public self-government will be established, a society in which labor for the good of society will become the prime vital requirement of everyone, a necessity recognized by one and all, and the ability of each person will be employed to the greatest benefit of all people.

As a statement of an ideal society it has much to recommend it, though it is obviously only partially and abstractly stated. A communist society is a classless, wealthy society in which the means of production are publicly owned and the people are fully developed, free, socially conscious, and dedicated to working for the good of all. As a movement, communism is humanistic because it has as its aim the production of this society which is said to be both the society all men desire and the most desirable of all societies. Unfortunately neither of these claims, which are often reiterated by Soviet Marxists, is ever submitted to analysis or defended in detail. They are taken as self-evident truths. The only question which does arise is how best and most quickly this society can be achieved.

Communism as an ideal, we have seen, is a complex whole. It is a society with certain characteristics, all of which were mentioned at one time or another by Marx. Each component is worthwhile in itself. But is the most desirable society one which has *these* components and not some other group? The Soviet line simply asserts that a communist society is one which has these traits, and that they adequately characterize the society. But since Marx admittedly could not foresee the future in any detail, a more plausible position is that though these are some traits of a communist society, it will also have a great many others which can be clarified only as the society approaches its realization. But this approach raises some difficult questions. For 1) how is anyone to tell which traits are proper for the society of the future? and 2) since we are talking of a whole in which various ingredients must be mixed, how are we to tell which of several wholes, all of which contain admirable traits, is superior?

To many Marxists both questions are pseudo-questions, since as the economic base of society develops, the organization of society will take place of its own accord. As the society becomes sufficiently rich to take care of the rational needs of the people, all men—providing there are no exploiters or ruling class—will receive what they need and live in peace, prosperity, and harmony.

This pat solution, however, does not fit either the facts of the development of Soviet society or the Marxist-Leninist claim that the key to the freedom of the new society is planning and not automatic development.

In the Party Program's definition of communism there was no mention of rights or of freedom of conscience or of artistic creativity. The chief components are wealth and social stability—components which some may wish to trade off against other values. Inherent in this view is the claim that there is one society which all men desire and that it will be achieved under the leadership of the party—if necessary despite the people's present wants—which rests secure in its paternalistic belief that this is best for all mankind.

The predominant justification of communism as an end has in the past been its inevitability. But as belief in the inevitability of communism has given way to the view that it must be built, a justification other than inevitability has been sought. What has been suggested by Soviet writers is that humanistic communism is the only society in which man's aims can be fulfilled, since in communism all is done for the sake of man and consequently communism is almost by definition what man seeks. If in fact many men do not presently seek it, they must be shown that they seek it implicitly; and the only ones who can reasonably oppose it are those who put their own good and desires above the general good and the desires of the majority. These are expendable, for communist humanism does not apply to all men, nor is it realized or realizable in the present. Communism is a humanism; but the communist movement is not. For only with the full realization of communism will full humanism be achieved.

Collectivism

The collectivist aspect of Soviet Marxist humanism does not appear explicitly in the Party Program definition of communism, but it permeates the Program and the pertinent Soviet literature. It follows as a corollary from the Soviet Marxist notion of man.

Man, as we have seen, is the ensemble of his social relations. He is wholly social and it is man as a social unit which is the object of Soviet humanism. Soviet humanism is to be achieved in the future and it is to be achieved on the social level. This means, according to Soviet theory, that man is to be made free by making society free, that man is to be made happy by making society happy. Freedom, happiness, and other noble qualities desired by man can be achieved only collectively, not piecemeal or individually. If man is to be changed by changing society, he is to be made human by making society humane. This is the collectivist aspect of Soviet Marxist humanism.

We can clarify the position by dealing specifically with the notions of happiness and freedom. Neither of these can correctly, according to the Soviet view, be considered from a personal point of view only. For happiness achieved or freedom exercised at another's expense cannot constitute true happiness or real freedom. Yet in a class society this is the only way that these qualities can supposedly be attained. The exploited and oppressed can scarcely be said to be either happy or free; and to the extent that the members of the exploiting class are either, they achieve their happiness or freedom at the expense of those whom they plunder either individually or as a class.

True freedom and happiness, the Marxist view continues, are only possible when the happiness and freedom of all become real possibilities, that is, when the happiness or the freedom of each does not hinder the happiness and freedom of others. Social conditions must promote general happiness and freedom, and this is only possible in a society in which there are no exploiters and in which personal and social interests coincide. Happiness and freedom in a dog-eat-dog society necessarily become the happiness and freedom of one individual at the expense of another. Where, however, everyone sees himself as part of the social whole and desires the social good, where he sees his own good and welfare of that whole, then the clash of personal interests is avoided. Genuine freedom and happiness therefore call for the proper organization of society and the proper education of its members.

Soviet Marxist writers thus emphasize the social aspects of happiness and freedom and their social conditions. This has been the basic component of Soviet Marxist humanism. Only recently have a few Soviet writers ventured beyond this basic position in their analysis of happiness and freedom.

V. P. Tugarinov, for one, distinguishes the objective conditions necessary for happiness (which he agrees are a classless society in which the happiness of each does not detract from but helps the happiness of others) from the subjective or individual use of the opportunities with which society provides its members.[1] Society, he realizes, cannot give anyone

happiness, nor he emphasizes, can any individual expect society to make him happy; society simply makes available the
prerequisites for happiness. The distinction between society's
supplying the conditions for happiness and an individual's
achieving personal happiness is an interesting one which, unfortunately, Tugarinov does not pursue. For him, as well as
for the other Soviet writers, the essential points are that no
one is to achieve happiness at the expense of another and that
society is to provide the objective conditions for individual
happiness—which includes training him to seek his own good
in the general good.

The analysis of individual freedom by Soviet Marxists is
not merely overshadowed by considerations of the social conditions of freedom but almost overwhelmed by them. A few
lines here and there are all that have yet become visible.

Society's freedom, it is claimed, is the prerequisite for the
exercise of individual freedom. Freedom in the Marxist view is
a function of knowledge. It consists of "insight into necessity."
Man is free when he is able to achieve what he strives to
attain, and this presupposes knowledge of the objective conditions of his activity and of the means necessary to achieve
his ends, as well as actually acting on this knowledge. It also
assumes that by so acting he will not produce any unexpected
results which could tend to thwart his present end, his future
ends, or those of anyone else. If I achieve what I desire at the
expense of another, then I achieve my freedom at his expense.

For the Soviet Marxist the true freedom of man consists
first of all in the members of a society having sufficient collective knowledge to organize the society so as to achieve its
collective goals and avoid producing results it does not desire.
Within this framework, if what each person desires coincides
with and does not interfere with the general good, then each
should be able to achieve his own particular ends without
interfering with the ends of another. Thus F. V. Konstantinov,
a leading Soviet philosopher, says, "Real freedom for the individual and society commences only after society has abandoned the realm of blind necessity and poverty dominated by
spontaneously acting social forces and has entered the realm of

freedom based on reason and on appropriate economic, social, political, and spiritual conditions of life, freedom to live and act for *all*, for the people and not just for the select few."[2] One of the few articles dealing in any detail with the personal aspect of freedom proceeds from the social conditions of freedom to the notion of an individual creatively, instead of mechanically, responding to his situation and initiating a new line of determination.[3] But the nature of this creativity, the way it is nurtured or developed, and the like, are never pursued or clarified.

Soviet Marxist humanism is a humanism of the future; the present attempts to produce it consist of attempts to produce a new society. Soviet Marxist humanism is collectivistic; it considers the components of this new society primarily in their social dimension and not in how they are to be developed or achieved on an individual level. These two components of communist humanism, however, are not necessarily the components of everything that goes by the name of "socialist humanism," despite the fact that socialist humanism also puts the emphasis on society and on changing social conditions in order to make the social order and men more human.

Those new Marxists who reject the collectivist and paternalistic aspect of the Soviet view of man similarly reject these components in their humanism. Some, like the Yugoslav philosopher Gajo Petrović, distinguish between a free society—in which not all perhaps are free—and a non-free society in which perhaps some are nonetheless free. In arguing for a free society of free persons, however, he emphasizes that "freedom cannot be given as a gift to or forced upon anyone. An individual becomes a free human person only through his own free activity."[4] The notion of autonomy which we saw earlier in relation to man is developed in this connection by these new Marxists. For a society cannot become free unless it contains free creative individuals, who must form themselves as well as creating for themselves the conditions for their freedom. Freedom and happiness are individually enjoyed, and though they are aided by social conditions, unless men constantly strive to achieve them in the present, they may well forget how to achieve them in the future.

Humanism and the Arts

Part of the Soviet Marxist humanist line consists in extolling the arts. If man's value consists in reflecting the riches of society, then he can be more of a person, a culturally richer person, the greater the culture of the society in which he lives. Soviet Marxists never tire of praising the development of the arts in the Soviet Union and of decrying the decadence, morbidity, sex-crazed state of the arts in the Western countries.

There is no doubt that in the Soviet Union some giant strides have been taken to disseminate both the appreciation and the practice of some of the arts. Music education, for instance, is government subsidized. Orchestras and opera, ballet and theatre companies and groups are found on all levels of community life and are widespread throughout the country. Soviet musicians and composers are well known throughout the world, as are some of their performers and writers. But paternalism infects the arts also. It is not the average participants or the general public who chafe under this artistic paternalism—for these recipients undoubtedly benefit. But many creative artists and writers seem less than content with the cultural norms established by the party in the name of the people.

The Soviet attitude toward art and culture in its creative dimension has vacillated during the years since 1917. Though initially a good deal of flexibility was allowed, the emphasis was always on the desirability of producing for the masses. The result was the dogmatization of what came to be known as socialist realism in all realms of artistic endeavor, and this was often interpreted according to the predilections of the leader in power—Lenin or Stalin or Khrushchev. Essentially art was to be not only intelligible to the masses but was to educate them, elevate them, and deepen their appreciation of the beauty, progressive spirit, and optimism of socialism. Since this didactic aim of the party did not always correspond with the artists' aim of artistic expression, censorship and tight controls over all artistic endeavors developed. Music in the twelve-tone idiom, jazz, abstractionism in painting and sculpture were all for long periods proscribed, and literature and poetry are still censored.

Since Khrushchev's fall from power the situation has eased somewhat. Controls are still enforced, but the rumbling from some of the artistic elements in the Soviet Union are growing louder. Jazz is tolerated; limited experiments using the twelve-tone scale have been made by composers; abstract art flourishes unofficially. The voice of the writers has been heard most clearly. Andrei A. Voznesensky, a Soviet poet, in a widely circulated letter which *Pravda* refused to publish, protested violently against the Union of Writers, saying, "Clearly the leadership of the Union does not regard writers as human beings. This lying, prevarication, and knocking people's heads together is standard practice."[5] Others spoke almost as strongly during and after the Daniel and Sinyavsky trials. The vocal artistic agitators are still a small minority; but the fact that they can speak with relative impunity itself indicates a change from the days of Stalin.

The official Soviet view of what constitutes good and appropriate literature, art, and music does not always coincide with what some of the creative artists think. And so far, in such disputes, it is the officials who win. This aspect of Soviet paternalism may become somewhat tempered. Only time will tell in the Soviet Union, though already in Poland, Hungary, Czechoslovakia, and Yugoslavia socialist realism has had its day and creative experimentation in the arts and literature, if not positively encouraged, is at least tolerated.

Humanism and Religion

Marxist humanism identifies itself with atheism. In this identification it associates itself with other types of humanism, which it claims to continue, complete, and bring down to earth from their former utopian and abstract state. By associating itself with atheism Marxist humanism claims that it is man-centered and not God-centered, that it strives for the benefit of man in this life and not in some future life-after-death, and that it frees man from the chains imposed upon him by religion and its ministers and priests. The Marxist position is based on a twofold claim. The first is that Marxism or Marxism-Leninism is scientific; its humanism is consequently based on science, which, according to the Soviet Marxists, has both disproved the existence of God and proven the truth of the claim that only matter exists and precedes thought or consciousness. Any being such as God is traditionally conceived to be—a spirit—is thus simply an impossibility. Secondly, Marxism claims to account for the origin of religion; in so doing it attempts both to show that religious faith is misplaced and to indicate that man's faith should be placed in man, where it properly belongs.

Prior to Marx the German philosopher Ludwig Feuerbach had attempted to show that religious worship was misdirected. Each man, he argued, compared himself with the abilities and feats of mankind in general, and found himself wanting. Men tended to form the conception of some superbeing who had all the perfections they lacked, and then started to treat this concept as if it really existed independently of themselves. If a man lacked knowledge, his super-being, whom he named God, became all-knowing; if he was weak, his God became all-powerful; if he was finite, his God became infinite, and so on. Men then fell down and worshiped this God whom they had conceived and objectified, failing to realize that it was their own creation.

This was Feuerbach's psychological explanation of religion. From it he drew the conclusion that man should not worship God but Man, that Theology should be replaced by Anthropology, that man should become the proper object of man's concern, and that humanism should become his religion.

Marx was influenced by this analysis of the origin of religion, but he considered the solution proposed by Feuerbach inadequate. Religion, in Marx's view, was the opium of the people. It helped them forget their misery, and gave them solace by offering them the false hope of happiness in a life-after-death. Such false beliefs and false hopes, however, were not simply the result of false concepts, and the antidote to the opium of religion was not merely to replace God with the equally abstract concept of Man. Rather the source of the false belief and hope had to be rooted out. The cure would follow automatically.

For Marx religion formed part of the superstructure of society. It was one of the ways in which the ruling class, through their witting or unwitting instruments—the priests and ministers—kept the people under control, content with their lot, and uninterested in revolution. The antidote for religion was thus social change. When there was no longer a ruling class the need for religion would die away and religious faith would go with it. When man saw things rightly because he had no reason to hide them from himself, when he was no longer oppressed, when he reached the stage of communism, then he would have no need for nor inclination toward the false beliefs of religion.

Marx was an atheist, but he was not a militant atheist. He did not fight religion, but rather thought that it would disappear of itself when its roots were cut at the social level. Lenin introduced militant atheism into Marxist thought. Even as late as 1922 in writing to the journal *Under the Banner of Marxism* he emphasized that the journal should be an organ of militant atheism, which "must devote a lot of space to atheist propaganda."

Fifty years after the October revolution, religious belief continues to flourish in a significant portion of the Soviet population despite the severe restrictions on any form of organized religion. During World War II the Russian Orthodox and a few other religious groups were granted organizational concessions because of the part they could play in helping to mobilize the population for the defense of the motherland against the invading German armies. But beginning again in 1959 anti-religious campaigns have increased in intensity. Only three Orthodox theological seminaries remain in the Soviet Union, and only three major Soviet cities—Odessa, Moscow, and Leningrad—still have rabbis. Yet despite the great attrition of religious institutions, there are indications that large numbers of believers, among whom are the

young and the male, as well as the old and the female, still
exist. The number also includes intellectuals, as Stalin's own
daughter, Svetlana Alliluyeva, testifies.

The attitude of the new Marxists toward religion seems
at best ambiguous. The theoreticians, as opposed to the militant, professional *antireligiozniki*, seem quite tolerant of religious belief, though not believers themselves. Indifference
rather than militant atheism seems to describe their attitude.
But there is a growing body of "scientific atheistic" literature,
most of it produced on orders from the party and its leaders.
Some writers have also felt compelled to attempt some sort
of explanation of the failure of religious belief to wither away
despite the establishment of a classless, socialist society.

The new Marxists of other countries of Eastern Europe
seem even more tolerant of or indifferent to religion and
religious belief. In most of these countries some form of
Christianity is still strongly embedded, though usually fought
at the organizational level by the communist party leaders of
the countries in question, who see organized religion as a
political threat to their own power. The actions of party
leaders notwithstanding, the writing of the new Marxists cannot be called militantly atheistic by any means, though they
champion a humanism which is atheistic, which sees man's
good as achievable in this life, and which regards religion
as a false, though not necessarily pernicious, belief.

Marxism and Alienation

At the heart of Marxist humanism is the doctrine of alienation. For it is by overcoming or doing away with his alienation
that man is supposed to find and realize his true self.

Marx presented his notion of alienation in most detail
in the posthumously published work given the name *Economic
and Philosophical Manuscripts of 1844*, though commentators
are now for the most part agreed that the idea, if not the
term, is to be found throughout his later works as well. For
Marx both man and society could be termed alienated, and
though one could speak of religious, political, social, and

other types of alienation, the basic type was economic alienation, especially the alienation of labor.

Alienation consists essentially of a separation or division
of what should be unified; it also consists in the reification of
abstractions or relations in such a way as to make them into
forces which dominate and limit their human creators. For
Feuerbach man made the concept of God into a real object
which he then bowed down before and which he allowed to
control and limit him. This for Feuerbach was the essence
of religious alienation, and religious de-alienation consisted
simply in reconceiving religion, in seeing its object as man,
and in becoming united with other men through love.

For Marx the essential alienation is economic and it can
be changed not by revising its concepts, but only by changing the existing economic order. Man for Marx was alienated
in three basic ways: the worker was alienated or separated
from the products of his labor, from his productive activity,
and from both other men (his species life) and nature. The
first type of alienation resulted from the fact that the products of a worker's labor, which are an extension of himself,
were in fact not his but another's, namely the entrepreneur's
for whom he worked. The alienation of the worker from the
products of his labor has several dimensions. Not only does
he produce products over which he has no subsequent control, but in general products or commodities in capitalist
society separate men instead of uniting them. Man works for
objects which he buys or covets. Instead of being simply
objects for men's use, they become symbols for which one
works, for which one lives, and the value of a person is judged
not by what he is but by what he owns. Man is not simply
separated from the objects of his labor, but the fight and
desire for them dominate him, instead of his dominating and
using the objects.

The alienation of man from his productive activity results
from the fact that men in a capitalist society have to sell
their time, their labor, in order to earn enough to live. But
labor, as we have seen, is man's essential activity. It is by
his labor that he expresses himself, that he differentiates him-

self from animals. Labor should therefore be an extension of oneself, a free satisfying expression of what one is. An example would be an artist who through his painting expresses what he is and feels, who lives to paint and finds enjoyment and fulfillment in painting. This is what labor should be. But in capitalist society Marx finds the laborer selling his labor to the entrepreneur. It no longer belongs to him but to another. And instead of expressing himself creatively in his labor he does the most tedious and stultifying of jobs. Instead of living to work, he works in order to live. He considers his working time not his own and not an expression of himself. Only his off hours are his. Those hours alone are when he is himself and owns himself; in his essential activity he is separated from himself and subservient to his work, which he must do to earn enough to keep himself alive.

The separation of man from other men and from nature is a necessary consequence. What is not mine is someone else's, whether it be the product of my labor or my labor time and activity. Ownership divides men and keeps them apart. The division is heightened by the fact that each individual in capitalist society becomes equated with his function. Each does his small job, and becomes that small job, because that is the way he expresses himself. The multidimensionality of society, the cultural wealth that it possesses is enjoyed by only a few, and even by them only in part. For, as we have already seen, if the essence of man is the ensemble of his social relations, a divided society produces an essence which cannot be enjoyed in its entirety by any of the members of the parts. In his individual existence each man lives in a fragmented way, separated from other men, and sharing or reflecting in only a portion of his true essence, the social relations of his society.

Marx's diagnosis of the ills of capitalist society are of course given in terms of what he envisages a total or human or healthy society to be. In it each man would express himself in a multiplicity of ways, and would freely engage in labor as an artist does. He would share what he produces with others as they with him. He would not be separated from his fellow men by goods, but all the products of labor would be kept in their proper place. Men would achieve their true stature, and economic activity would consist of the control and manipulation of goods and not of people. The divisions of society would thus fall away. Man would no longer be separated from other men by goods or rank or class. All men would freely and creatively express themselves and develop themselves. The essence of man could then be enjoyed equally (within the capacity of each) and fully by each man in his individual existence. And with the end of economic alienation, all the other types of alienation—social, political, ideological— would wither away.

The key to the de-alienation of capitalist society and of the men who inhabit it lay for Marx in the abolition of the private ownership of the means of production, of the division of labor, and of the existence of classes. All three, moreover, in his view were interrelated and would have to be eliminated together. The proletarian revolution was the means he envisaged for accomplishing this. For with the triumph of the proletariat, classes would be abolished. There would be no dominating and dominated. The means of production would be commonly owned, so no one would own the labor of another or hold it within his power to decide whether to let another work or not, and so live or not. Exploitation would thus be ended. Together with this men could express themselves freely in their own work, laboring together and sharing the products of their labor, taking part in management as well as in more routine tasks, governing themselves because there would be no governing class. They would thus lead full and varied lives in the new classless society, and true humanism would be achieved.

Lenin's revolution was a success. The means of production were taken over by the state in the name of all the people. The exploitation (employment) of one individual by another was ended. Classes were officially done away with. Has alienation therefore ended in the Soviet Union?

The answer given by most Soviet writers on the topic is a qualified "yes"; that given by the more outspoken new

Marxists of Poland, Yugoslavia, and Hungary is a resounding "no."

According to the Soviet position alienation in the sense in which Marx used the term, the alienation characteristic of capitalistic bourgeois society, has been essentially done away with in the Soviet Union. This follows almost by definition since officially there are no more classes, and in fact there is no private ownership of the means of production. Men are supposedly no longer dominated by goods or by the economy. Soviet society is thus not alienated, it is claimed, though some men within that society may still not be fully integrated. Communism, says Professor T. I. Oiserman of Moscow State University, does away with antagonistic contradictions, and though other kinds of contradiction remain—between the old and new, subjective and objective—these cannot be given the name "alienation." "The latter," he claims, "has a definite meaning which is lost if the attempt is made to make it absolute, universal and stretch it to cover all conceivable things."[6]

Though private ownership of the means of production and classes have been officially done away with in the Soviet Union the presence of the division of labor causes the Soviet Marxists some concern. Most, like N. F. Naumova, would admit that it is impossible to provide creative labor for all members of society, and that division of labor continues to exist.[7] What they deny, however, is that this results in alienation. The solutions given are varied. They claim on the one hand that the worker in Soviet society knows why he is working, realizes his role and function in society, and feels himself performing his social duty. This does or at least can eliminate the sense of separation a laborer at work in a capitalist society feels. The social worker is working for himself and his fellow men, not for an exploiter, even if his job is routine. On the other hand the claim is made in different ways that eventually the division of labor—at least in its negative characteristics—will be overcome by shortening the working day, by combining productive work with public administration, art, and so on, by increasing education and facilitating movement from one job to another, and by other similar means.

The non-Soviet new Marxists, however, are not by any means so sanguine about the absense of alienation either in the Soviet Union or in other socialist countries. They claim both that the old types of alienation characteristic of capitalist society have not been overcome, and that new types of alienation have sprung up in socialist society itself.

As to the first point, the discussion hinges on whether socialist society is truly classless or whether in fact a new class of leaders has arisen—the managerial class, which though it does not own the means of production does in fact control both them and the workers. In Marx's view, they argue, the means of production were to be owned by all in common; but in the Soviet Union private ownership has been replaced by state ownership or state capitalism, which is as exploitative as private ownership was. In essence, then, neither class division, nor private ownership of the means of production, nor the division of labor has actually been overcome. Consequently alienation still remains within Soviet society, though perhaps in a more attenuated form than in capitalist countries.

The accusation that socialism produces its own forms of alienation has caused quite a stir in some countries of Eastern Europe, and it has provoked a good deal of official comment. One case in point is the inhospitable reaction of the leaders of the Polish Communist Party to Adam Schaff's claims in *Marxism and the Individual* that political alienation will remain in socialism as long as the state, which is an instrument of coercion, remains. When the people do not control and rule themselves, they are ruled and controlled by another. Privilege, status, the distinction of ruler and ruled similarly tend to separate men from men and fragment society.

Other Marxists go still further. Predrag Vranicki, a professor at the University of Zagreb, claims "practical experience has shown that many deforming aspects of alienation are possible under socialism."[8] The presence of a market economy, of money, of a state, of a hierarchy of states, of a division into the public and personal components of life are all, he claims, aspects of alienation which are yet to be overcome. Miklos Almasi provoked a general discussion of alienation among Hungarian Marxists by an article in the *New Hungarian Quarterly* on "Alienation and Socialism." [9] There he claimed that the sources of alienation in socialist society stemmed from personality cults and the power of leaders, from over-centralization and the overexpansion of the state, from the separation of public and private life, and from the continued division of labor. The "creative Marxists" of *Praxis*, together with their defense of self-management socialism point to bureaucracy as one of the sources of alienation in socialism. But the general view of all these Marxists seems to be that though alienation remains in socialist society, socialism and communism in some form offer a solution to it. Capitalism, on the other hand, is eternally trapped in alienation and offers no way out.

Two statements concerning alienation deserve mention be-cause they indicate the beginning of a new analysis. One is by a Hungarian philosopher and follower of Georg Lukács, Agnes Heller. In analyzing the problem of alienation from the "structure of everyday life" she asserts that regardless of the socio-economic condition of his society, it is possible for an individual to overcome his own alienation. [10] The standard Marxist position seemed to be that while personal alienation was possible in a de-alienated society, the reverse was not the case. Miss Heller has now claimed the reverse is possible as well. The Yugoslav philosopher Gajo Petrović also offers a new interpretation of alienation by considering man's essence "a set of historically created human possibilities" from which "at any given state of his evolution (even at the most ad-vanced one) man can be alienated from it, i.e., below the level of his possibilities." [11] As a result, de-alienation for Petrović is always a relative term; communism will therefore at best be not a completely de-alienated society, but a "basi-cally nonalienated" one.

Marxist humanism is closely linked with the claim of over-coming the alienation of capitalist society. But the ambiguous status of alienation, which still clearly requires extensive analysis, tends to weaken to some extent its humanistic claims.

Marxism and Existentialism

The debates about alienation arose in Eastern Europe only after the question of alienation had already been raised anew by existentialism. Existentialism—especially the works of Martin Heidegger and Jean-Paul Sartre—hit the satellite countries of Eastern Europe with considerable force as of 1956. For the existentialists alienation was not an economic phenomenon so much as a condition of man in his finitude. Their humanism consisted not in changing the economic structure of society, but in emphasizing the uniqueness and importance of the individual in an impersonal, mechanized, bureaucratic society.

Adam Schaff summarizes the situation in Poland neatly. Existentialism had become popular in Western Europe after World War II because it raised problems connected with the individual and his fate, with death, with the meaning of life, with the validity of traditional culture and values, with the helplessness of the individual before overwhelming social and political and economic forces, with the meaning of individual responsibility, and so on. In February 1956 at the end of the Twentieth Party Congress of the Soviet Union Khrushchev made his speech denouncing the Stalinist personality cult. Stalin, who previously had been hailed as the great renowned leader of all workers, was denounced for the use of "violence, mass repressions, and terror," for mistakes and crimes. The revelation shook communist believers deeply, and the mark was made even deeper by the brutal repression of the Hungarian uprising by Soviet troops and tanks, and by the social unrest in Poland, Germany, and elsewhere. Schaff writes:

> These factors acted all the more forcefully under the specific conditions in Poland after 1956. Here we had not only a general undermining of criteria of judgment, not only a widespread crisis of values and a feeling of the insecurity of one's fate and of the senselessness of conscious activity, the usual accompaniments of stormy periods of wars and revolutions. There arose in our country, at least among certain circles, an even fiercer

storm. The disclosure by the international communist movement of what we call in our jargon "mistakes and distortions"
was for many a moral and political earthquake. . . .

Is there anything strange in the fact that those who formerly
submitted blindly to all orders because they believed in their
correctness should, in the face of revealed abuses, now raise
questions about the individual's responsibility for his actions
and the conflict between conscience and discipline? Is it surprising that such people should raise questions about the role
of the individual in the mass movement, and about how he is to
decide for himself in the case of conflicts between what he is
called upon to do and his own standards of right and wrong? . . .

Is it surprising, then, that people turned to sources where
they could find some sort of analysis of the problems perplexing
them . . . ? No, it is sad that they turned to Existentialism, with
its negative outlook, but fully understandable.[12]

Schaff concludes by claiming that the Marxists, who had ignored the problems of the individual, must turn their attention
to these problems and supply their own solutions, since Marxism
and existentialism, the one emphasizing the individual and the
other emphasizing society, are ultimately incompatible.

The existentialist-Marxist debate had actually begun in Western Europe at least as early as 1945. Jean-Paul Sartre, Maurice
Merleau-Ponty, and Albert Camus—all of whom admitted to
varying degrees the importance of Marxism to Western thought
and yet were in some sense allied with what has become known
as existentialism—were on one side. Lesser known French thinkers—H. Lefebvre, P. Naville, R. Garaudy and others defended
"modern" Marxism or Marxism-Leninism as best they could. But
they were hopelessly outclassed. Georg Lukács, the well-known
Hungarian Marxist, entered the fray with a book entitled *Exis-
tentialisme ou Marxisme?* in 1948, and it appeared that a dialogue would develop. For Lukács was sympathetic to Marx's
early humanistic writings and to the problems that the existentialists were dealing with. He also brought a new dimension to
the debate by turning his attention to the nineteenth-century
father of phenomenology, Edmund Husserl, and to Heidegger.
Lukács' characterization of existentialism as a philosophy which
represented the spiritual and moral chaos of the contemporary

intelligentsia, as a glorification of the isolated individual, and as a passive nihilistic doctrine opposed to social action, became the standard Marxist interpretation of the movement.

The debate continued, developed, and changed. Merleau-Ponty and Albert Camus died. Lukács turned his attention elsewhere. The works of Sartre, Camus, and Heidegger were brought into Eastern Europe and read. Interest grew. Following the events of 1956, Sartre was asked to write an article on existentialism for the Polish journal *Tworczosc*. His contribution appeared in 1957. Instead of attacking Marxism, Sartre defended his own interpretation of Marxism against its moribund interpreters. Though Marxism presents the only true philosophy of history, it fails to present a satisfactory human anthropology. Sartre suggests that existentialism can add this, not replacing but supplementing Marxism. Schaff in a series of articles rose to reply and not only declined to accept Sartre's suggestion but argued for the basic incompatibility of Marxism and existentialism. Nonetheless a number of East European intellectuals paid more than passing attention to the writings of the existentialists, and a number have been deeply influenced by them. The impact of existentialism was greater on the dramatists and novelists than on the philosophers, though on some younger philosophers it has been considerable.

Soviet philosophers, shielded from the realities of the Western world, were long in noticing existentialism and even longer in joining the fray. They have remained primarily on the sidelines, and cannot be said to have taken part in a dialogue of any sort. They condemn existentialism as they condemn all of Western philosophy. Though there are some indications that some Soviet philosophers are reading the existentialist philosophers more closely than before, their critical articles remain for the most part standard refutations and rebuttals.[13] Yet even in the Soviet Union some unpublished writers and philosophers are alleged to have been influenced by the existentialists, and the published philosophers have acknowledged that there are problems concerning the individual and his fate and concerning values which have not been adequately dealt with by Marxists and which deserve attention.

The details of the controversy between Sartre and the Marxists need not detain us here. For it seems that the former dogmatic, entrenched positions of both are now things of the past. What is significant is not so much their differences, as the ways in which Sartre's Marxist existentialism and the existentialized Marxism of some of the new Marxists, especially those of Poland, Yugoslavia, and Czechoslovakia, resemble each other. It is no longer a matter of "either/or," of a choice between Marxism and existentialism. Both Marxists and existentialists raise similar problems and both search for adequate solutions.

The basic thrusts of Sartre and of such new Marxists as Leszek Kolakowski of Poland, Karel Kosík of Czechoslovakia, and of some of the "creative Marxists" of Yugoslavia's *Praxis* seem similar. All oppose dogmatic Marxism; all submit socialist as well as capitalist society to critical scrutiny; all find alienation in both Eastern and Western societies and deplore bureaucracy and other restrictions on man's freedom and creativity; all envisage a society of free, autonomous individuals and reject the collectivist Soviet vision of man; all wrestle with the problem of individual responsibility and with an individual's responsibility for history as well as for himself, though they realize that the individual in industrialized society tends to become a cog in the machine.

Existentialism served to raise questions which Marxism had previously ignored. The anthropological emphasis of many of the new Marxists coincides with the emphasis of existentialism on the individual, and the latter certainly has helped encourage the former. There is still much of existentialism that is ignored by the new Marxists, and there are many questions raised by the existentialists—including the meaning of death—which the new Marxists have yet to raise seriously. But that there is a positive ferment among at least some of the new Marxists with respect to the perennial philosophical questions concerning the individual and his place in the universe cannot be denied, though it is weaker in the Soviet Union than in some other countries of Eastern Europe.

Soviet humanism and socialist humanism are both offered as the solution to man's ills. Both emphasize the fundamental modification of society. The one places its emphasis on the future, the other worries about the present as well. Both moreover claim to be the moral as well as the practical answer to man's unhappy condition, and so it is to an examination of Marxist ethics and communist morality that we now turn.

5

Marxist Ethics
and Communist Morality

■ Karl Marx left no single work which is dedicated either in whole or in any substantial part to questions of ethics, though his works are replete with moral judgments and moral indignation. Attempts to construct or to reconstruct Marx's ethical position have led to a number of controversial presentations by Western scholars, most of which lean heavily on his earlier more philosophical writings. All of them involve a patchwork process and an elaborate exegesis of Marx's works, and none of them has been completely successful in its endeavor.

Engels' contribution to the field of ethics is more direct than Marx's. But even Engels presents only the embryonic beginnings of a Marxist ethics in his criticism of other ethical systems in *Anti-Dühring* and *Ludwig Feuerbach*. Lenin rarely deals with ethics, and his most sustained effort is his short speech on the "Tasks of the Youth Leagues" in which he defines morality as "what serves to destroy the old exploiting society" and to build up "a new, communist society." If to this meager inheritance from the Marxist-Leninist classics we add the fact that many Marxists felt that morality, being part of the superstructure, would take care of itself as the economic base of society changed, we can understand the paucity of later Marxist writings on ethics. The few that did appear were primarily by revisionists of the late nineteenth century or of the 1920's, who turned to

Kant or to Nietzsche, or to other philosophers, to fill the Marxian ethical void.

By the early part of the 1950's, however, it had become obvious that the moral customs of the Soviet people had not changed significantly, despite the change in the Soviet social structure and in the means and modes of production and ownership which had been brought about since the revolution of 1917. This, together with other secondary causes (such as the toleration of more philosophical discussion by Soviet leaders) has led to the rapid development of a quite voluminous body of Soviet literature on ethics and morality and to the official promulgation in 1961 of a "Moral Code of the Builder of Communism." Thus for the first time we have the emergence of an orthodox Marxist-Leninist ethics, authorized and approved by the Communist Party of the Soviet Union.

This Marxist-Leninist ethics, however, is racked by a twofold tension. The first arises from the nature of ethics itself, insofar as it is a theory of morals. For as a philosophical theory it is concerned with conceptual clarity and precision and with logical coherence and consistency. But insofar as it is concerned with morality, it becomes involved with the practical ends of morality, which include social control and the maintenance of social order. The elucidation of a morality suited to promoting order in socialist society and to facilitating control by its leaders is the primary task which has been assigned to and undertaken by Soviet moral philosophers.[1] The fulfillment of this task, however, is not always consistent with the search for clarity and consistency, and with the necessity of following an argument wherever it leads. This tension is not peculiar to Soviet ethics. In the past it has led some Western philosophers to promote socially disruptive views, to champion reforms in social practices or organization, or to present what seemed to them higher or more consistent norms than those which were being generally followed. It might well lead others to divorce themselves from a study of the content of morality and to concentrate exclusively on what has come to be called meta-ethics, or the study of the language, structure, and logic of ethics and of moral reasoning as such. Neither path, however, is open to the

Soviet moral philosopher. For the former, being disruptive of social order, is tantamount to treason; and the latter involves avoiding his primary task.

The second tension arises from the fact that the Soviet moral philosopher is forced to work within the framework of the Marxist-Leninist classics, which are fraught with contradictions. The early works of Marx pull in the direction of humanism and freedom, the later works in the direction of economism and social engineering; the dialectic pushes one way and materialism another; Marx championed the proletariat, Lenin the vanguard of the proletariat or the party. Since neither Marx nor Lenin presented a clear or fully developed ethical position, a creative approach is demanded in the construction of a Marxist-Leninist ethics; but ethics, like all philosophy, is considered an ideological tool in the Soviet Union, and surveillance of a political ideologist is unlikely to foster the creativity of a Soviet moral philosopher.

I shall first sketch the development of Soviet ethics in the light of Western ethics, and then characterize the content of the new, communist morality which is being preached, if not necessarily practiced. Following this I shall discuss briefly the ethical literature in other East European countries.

Marxist Ethical Theory: The Soviet Model

Soviet ethical theory is essentially monolithic. Though differences appear among the various Soviet writers on ethics, depending on the interpretation they give to one or another aspect of this theory, and also to some extent on their form of expression and development, they all accept the same basic position in ethics. Though one may emphasize the dialectical dualities of ethics—its objective and subjective, relative and absolute, temporal and eternal, class-bound and universal moments or aspects—and another the dependence of morality on economic conditions, the resulting disputes are minor compared to the vast area of agreement. It is therefore possible to characterize Soviet ethics as a whole, both as to method and as to what Soviet philosophers consider ethics to be.

Soviet or Marxist-Leninist ethics at least nominally goes back to Marx. It should not, therefore, be surprising if it resembles the ethical theory of the nineteenth century more closely than that of the twentieth century in Western Europe and America. Simply stated it is metaphysically based, teleologically oriented, and objectivist in its claims.

(1) To say that Soviet ethics is "metaphysically based" is merely to say that it depends on certain premises or claims which it is beyond the province of ethics to establish, and that these premises are non-empirical insofar as they cannot be proved by means of the positive sciences. Soviet ethics is of course not unique in this and it shares this characteristic with Christian, Hegelian, and other ethical positions.

Soviet ethics is thus not an independent discipline but is based upon and is inextricably bound up with the teachings of historical materialism. From this it takes both the premise that history is developing in a certain direction and the premise that the end toward which it is developing is communism. Since morality is a form of social consciousness, what is true of the other forms (law, religion, politics, etc.) is true of it also. Since capitalism is dying and communism will eventually triumph everywhere and perpetually, capitalist or bourgeois morality is also said to be dying and communist morality, it is claimed, will be the morality of the future.

Whether the Soviet claims are either valid or proved is not at issue here. The dependence of Soviet ethics on certain claims of historical materialism is openly admitted and these claims serve as a methodological guide for Soviet moral philosophers. Bourgeois morality is scrutinized to illustrate, not substantiate, the thesis that bourgeois society is decadent and dying. The premise need not be substantiated by the moralist because it is taken as proved by historical materialism. Soviet writers have admittedly had little difficulty finding decadent aspects of bourgeois life. But its positive aspects are ignored. On the other hand, positive aspects of Soviet life are extolled while negative aspects are explained away as the result of the "remnants of capitalism" which still exist in the Soviet Union.

(2) Soviet ethics, like utilitarianism, is teleological. As in utilitarianism, an act is judged by the goodness or badness of its consequences, and duty is defined in terms of goodness. Thus, generally speaking, the Soviets hold that an action is right insofar as it tends to produce a good result. However, here they depart from utilitarianism, for they say that good is neither equivalent to pleasure (as Bentham and Mill would hold) nor indefinable (as G. E. Moore and many following him today would contend). Since the *de facto* end of mankind is said to be communism, communism is equated to the greatest good or final moral end of mankind.

Soviet ethics can also be characterized as a self-realization type of morality, providing the self to be realized is mankind as a whole. In each stage of his development what is moral is a function of what is possible for mankind at that stage. Those actions which can be taken and which tend to produce or promote man's full development in a communist society are good or right. Those actions which tend to hinder this development are bad or wrong, as are those acts of omission which occur when men do not take advantage of the possibilities afforded them.

In either case Soviet ethics is teleological in the sense that it claims that a tendency to produce communism, which it equates to man's highest moral ideal, is the ultimate criterion of moral goodness. Soviet moral philosophers are, moreover, outspoken naturalists. They are aware of G. E. Moore's arguments against naturalism, but they reject them as word play and empty analysis devoid of content.

(3) In opposition to both continental and Anglo-American forms of subjectivism, the Soviets claim that in the criterion of communism, an objective norm, they have a valid (and the only valid) basis for making objective moral judgments about the rightness or wrongness, goodness or badness, of an act. The objective goodness or badness of an act, they claim, is a quality which that act possesses whether or not the quality in question is recognized or acknowledged. One's attitude toward a given act may be either positive or negative, and one may think the act is either right or wrong. But neither one's attitude toward it

nor one's evaluation of the act determines its rightness or wrongness. If it leads to communism, it is right; if it hinders the march to communism, it is wrong. And presumably every act which one might wish to evaluate from the moral point of view does one or the other of these things, though the relation of many acts to the production of communism may seem tenuous and obscure, to say the least.

The Soviets deny any sharp distinction between fact and value, theory and practice, form and content. They claim that the terms of each of the pairs are always interrelated and consequently that no one can fruitfully separate or analyze them. Form without content is empty, content without form is unintelligible. Facts or states of affairs or actions are seen to have value or to lack it only when they are placed in the full context of a teleologically developing society.

To characterize Soviet ethics as metaphysical, teleological, naturalistic, and objectivistic is not necessarily to disparage it, though surely it does so in the eyes of some contemporary moral philosophers. It does, however, roughly place it in the spectrum of ethical positions. With this general orientation, let us turn to the Soviet concept of what ethics is and to an examination of its method.

Ethics, generally speaking, is held by the Soviets to be the science of morals.[2] More particularly it is concerned with the origin and development of morality, with the development of the principles and norms of communist morality and with the means of implementing them in Soviet life. Soviet writers reject the division of ethics into normative ethics on the one hand and critical ethics or meta-ethics on the other. For such a division separates theory from practice and form from content, which they claim are dialectically interrelated. Yet we can distinguish five different kinds of activity present in Soviet ethical writings, which in the absence of any Soviet terminology we can designate as description, interpretative classification, prescription, content-analysis, and refutation.

(1) *Description.* Every society develops certain customs, norms of action, and rules which help its members live together in comparative peace and cooperation. Some of the more impor-

tant customs become moral rules and carry with them the sanction of public opinion and sometimes of individual conscience.
The study of different moral systems and codes forms the descriptive portion of Soviet ethics. Here it depends upon the empirical findings of the historian, the anthropologist, the psychologist, or the sociologist—or on the characterizations of capitalist
society by Marx and Engels. The well-known differences among
different peoples are duly noted by the Soviets and taken as
evidence that the content of morality is not absolute or eternal,
but developing and changing. Actual studies of the morality
either of contemporary bourgeois or of Soviet society, detailed
descriptions of the norms actually followed, the values actually
held, are lacking, due among other reasons to the embryonic
state of sociological investigation in the Soviet Union. But Soviet moral philosophers, at least in theory, emphasize the importance of such studies.[3]

(2) *Interpretative classification.* Close upon this empirical study
comes the interpretative aspect of Soviet ethics which is concerned with the theoretical framework into which the empirical
findings are to be fitted. This interpretative classification constitutes the first part of its theory of morals. Its classification
system is for all practical purposes completed and no longer
discussed in the Soviet ethical literature, since it is taken over
from the doctrines of historical materialism.

Moral systems vary, it is held, because economic conditions
and conditions of life vary. Each group adopts those norms or
rules as moral which tend to promote its interests and aims.
In a society divided into classes, however, the interests and
aims of the different classes differ. The morality of the rulers
becomes the dominant morality, the one taught in the schools
and churches, though not necessarily the one people live by.
This morality protects the interests of the rulers and usually
aims at defending the *status quo*. The function of morality in a
class society is to defend the position and actions of the ruling
or dominant class and to keep the dominated subservient. Morality changes as economic and social conditions change. Slave-
holding morality was replaced by feudal morality, which in turn
was replaced by bourgeois morality. Bourgeois morality will

in turn be replaced by proletarian morality, in which the aims of all mankind (instead of the aims of some particular class) will at last be expressed. Thus the Soviets not only explain the origins and development of morality in the past, but they also chart its progress into the future. As common to all moral systems, moreover, they recognize certain simple norms of conduct which are necessary to the functioning of any society.

The above framework is sketched only in general terms. Some specific examples are given, for example, that slavery, which Aristotle defended as natural and therefore moral, came to be condemned as immoral once it became economically unprofitable. But no detailed attempt has been made either in the Marxist-Leninist classics or in the Soviet literature to relate the moral system of any society to the supposedly determinative economic conditions, or changes in the moral system to changing economic conditions.

(3) *Prescription.* From the basic empirical studies and the interpretative classification of Soviet ethics we proceed to the prescriptive or normative aspect of Soviet ethics. This consists of a systematic presentation of the content of socialistic and communistic morality, based on the socialist economic conditions of the USSR and the needs of Soviet society in its drive toward full-scale communism. The bulk of Soviet ethical writings falls into this class and consists of explaining the content of Soviet morality and of discussing how this new morality can be most effectively inculcated in the Soviet people. The greatest part of the Soviet ethical literature is consequently moralistic in nature, prescribing and promoting certain approved types of behavior. Thus Soviet moral philosophers do openly and primarily what they claim other philosophers do surreptitiously: they promote and defend the morality of the rulers or leaders of society, though they claim that in the instance of the Soviet Union the aims and good of the rulers coincide with those of the people.

The content of their moralizing we shall consider in the next part of this chapter.

(4) *Content-analysis.* Meta-ethics is conspicuously absent from the Soviet ethical literature. This results in part because

Soviet epistemology and semantics are in a state of chaos, and in part, if Soviet moral philosophers are to be taken at their word, because they consider conceptual analysis (of such terms as "good," "right," "responsibility," etc.) and such considerations as the logical justification of value judgments—which constitute the bulk of Anglo-American discussions in ethics—to be abstract and irrelevant inasmuch as they prescind from any particular content. Soviet moral philosophers do, however, engage in the discussion of what they call "ethical categories," and the most lively Soviet discussion in ethics during the past few years has centered on how the categories should be approached and how one should go about deciding whether, for instance, "justice" is a basic ethical category or not. There is as yet no resolution of this or similar questions.

A number of Soviet moral philosophers have discussed "good," "happiness," "honor," and "conscience" (the basic categories of ethics according to Soviet writers), as well as the concept of morality itself. Their approach is neither one of linguistic analysis nor of phenomenological description. "Content-analysis" perhaps describes most closely what they attempt to do. Characteristically this consists of an examination of the bourgeois, religious, or class content of these categories (what, for instance, Christian morality claims is good, what hedonism claims is good, etc.) followed by an exposition of the socialist content of these categories (e.g. what socialist morality claims is good). In some instances, however, they go beyond this to an analysis of a given concept's role, its subjective and objective character, and its relation to other concepts. The exact nature of the analysis involved is never clearly specified. In analyzing duty, for instance, we "see" that it plays the role of an ideal, of a norm, of a motive, and of a criterion of moral evaluation. What we look at in the analysis of each of these roles is not language, nor the idea alone, nor empirical descriptions of what people say they do, or of what they do, but all of these indiscriminately taken together. For all of them together make up the concept's content. Here above all there is room and need for philosophical development in

Soviet ethics; Soviet moral philosophers could learn much in this area from contemporary Western ethical writings.

The justification of morality as such is considered superfluous, since the existence of morality is a given fact. What is required is not justification but inculcation. The psychology of morals in the Western sense of the term is virtually nonexistent. Moral freedom is considered not on the level of individual action but on the level of social opportunities; guilt and shame have not been discussed, and conscience is considered only as a social phenomenon which is to be correctly molded. The philosophical considerations of the psychology of morals are glossed over and referred to the social psychologist, who is enjoined to find ways of motivating citizens to do willingly what is required of them.[4]

(5) *Refutation.* If the bulk of Soviet ethical writings is prescriptive or normative, the second largest class of articles is devoted to refutation. In the ideological struggle the refutation of bourgeois ethical theories—pragmatism, positivistism, emotivism, existentialism, neo-Thomism, and every other variety of (in Soviet parlance) idealistic ethics—is a paramount task imposed by the Party on its moral philosophers.[5] Scarcely an important Western book or article goes unrefuted, though the refutations are stereotyped, often polemical, and generally in terms of the accepted truths of Marxism-Leninism. Articles of this kind, however, are improving. More Soviet philosophers than heretofore seem to be reading carefully the Western works they criticize. They also adopt, adapt, and sometimes quote the criticism of one Westerner by another. No Soviet-Western dialogue has developed out of the Soviet criticisms, perhaps because they are rarely read and even more rarely answered by Western philosophers. But there are signs—still too few and too insignificant to make any conclusive judgment—that continued exposure may stimulate Soviet ideas which might be relevant to Western ethical thought. Western replies to Soviet criticism might well provide cross-fertilization between what are now separate and self-satisfied trends of thought.

Soviet Morality

While Soviet ethics seems to have little to say to Western philosophers along the lines of their primary concerns, Soviet morality may be of broader interest. For, in the first place, it is in many respects different from the moralities current in the West, and against it one may test or possibly enlarge one's own moral views. Secondly, if the Soviet Union successfully inculcates its moral values in its people, values held by a large proportion of the population of a continually shrinking world will certainly be a matter of interest.

The 1961 Party Program of the Communist Party of the Soviet Union promulgated the "Moral Code of the Builder of Communism," a list of twelve basic principles which every Soviet citizen is to cultivate—and which he is to see that everyone else cultivates.[6] The official promulgation of a moral code is something of an anomaly in modern times. Yet never before has a government so insistently demanded morality in all aspects of its citizens' lives, and then gone on to prescribe what that morality is to be. The code and the subsequent intensive publicity and explanation it has received in books, manuals on ethics, articles in the press and in popular and scholarly journals represent a major effort in the Government's program of molding the Soviet people for the future. It is an attempt on the part of Soviet leaders to use morality to supplement law and force; and if successful, the new morality may eventually replace the rule of force as a means of social control and provide the basis for social stability.

The production of social stability and order has always been one of the functions of morality. Another has often been social control. But in Western thought these have in the more enlightened systems been linked with a strong desire to preserve the sanctity of the individual conscience, and to foster the development of the individual moral person, who not only internalizes the moral norms of his society in the form of a superego but also reflects upon them and in a Kantian sense becomes an autonomous individual. Hegel differentiated between the unreflective, customary ethical life *(sittlich)* and the reflective moral life *(Moralität)*, and he considered the latter more advanced than the former. Bergson distinguished between social, closed morality and human, open morality, and considered the latter in some sense preferable. In the Soviet view, however, all such distinctions will be overcome in communist morality "which is the noblest and most just morality,"[7] and there will in fact be only public, social, unreflected, and closed morality. For the ultimate norm is not personal but social (the achievement of communism), the basic moral choice is not personal but social, the ultimate court of appeal is not one's conscience but society's decision. The ideal moral agent portrayed by Soviet morality is not the autonomous individual but the social conformist who actively participates in the struggle for achieving the aims of communist society.

An analysis of the new Soviet moral code reveals five distinctive features: (1) the ultimate guide and guardian of morality is the communist party; (2) communist morality is essentially a work morality; (3) it is an exclusively social morality; (4) it is a completely externalized morality; and (5) it is an inherently provincial morality.

(1) The twelve principles of communist morality promulgated by the communist party in effect replace the Ten Commandments which Moses received from God. The first of the twelve calls not for the worship of God but for "devotion to the communist cause; love of the socialist motherland and of the other socialist countries." We have seen that in communist morality what is good is equivalent to what leads to the ideal society, or to communism. But what leads to this end is determined by those who are leading the socialist society toward this end, namely the communist party in general and its leaders in particular. The leaders of the communist party are thus the champions and guardians of morality. As a consequence, moreover, the political and moral ends of Soviet society are said to coincide. What is required by Soviet law is *ipso facto* required by Soviet morality, and Soviet foreign policy, being a means of achieving communism, is automatically sanctified as moral and deserving of the moral support of the people. Since the communist party and its leaders determine both morality and poli-

tics, the party claims its actions have moral-political unity. Whatever the party does is thus by definition moral. There is no law of reason or of God above it, no higher court of appeal.

(2) If the end of communist morality and society is the achievement of communism, the means is work. Communism can be achieved only in a highly developed and highly productive society; for only in such a society will it be possible to give to each according to his need, even if this need be determined not by himself but by some norm supplied by something like a state. The goods which men need must be produced, and their production requires work.

Thus, in the Soviet Union, work is not only a physical necessity; it is raised to a moral obligation. The moral code in its second principle demands "conscientious labor for the good of society—he who does not work, neither shall he eat." To be moral is to work. All work is to be looked upon as dignified, and the meaning is given to all work done for the good of society and so for the eventual triumph of communism. Because work is so considered, negligence at work is tantamount to sabotage, and tardiness—which slows down or impairs production— a quasi-criminal act.[8]

Work discipline is now taught as a moral virtue; to be moral means to fulfill and overfulfill the State plans, to be careful of tools and materials at work, to treasure each minute at work, and to use each minute as efficiently as possible. There should be no envy at the success of another in his work, for his success is society's success; his increased production brings all the members of society a step closer to the common goal.

Work, as we have seen, has always held a central position in Marxist thought. It is by labor, according to Engels, that man distinguished himself from the brute and so became man. It is by his labor that man has changed and progressed, that he has developed from the caveman to the man of today. It is accordingly by labor—labor in collectives, labor for the socialist motherland, labor carried on diligently for the achievement of communism—that, according to the Soviets, the new man of Soviet society will be formed.

(3) The third outstanding feature of the moral code is that it presents an exclusively social morality, not a personal or individual one. It is socialized in that all one's duties come from society and all one's duties are toward society. The individual is enjoined not to think of himself except in his relation to society. Thus, the third principle calls for "concern on the part of everyone for the preservation and growth of public wealth"; the fourth for "a high sense of public duty; intolerance of actions harmful to the public interest"; the fifth for collectivism. The good of society, and not the good of any individual, is important and of moral concern; what is good for society is moral, what harms society is immoral. This has been carried to such an extent that offenses against social property have been punished by death; offenses against personal property, and even against individual persons, on the other hand, are not so harshly dealt with. To steal from an individual harms that individual; but to steal from society harms all individuals, since they make up society. Such actions are the more intolerable because they are claimed to be "remnants of capitalism." Similarly "careerism" and "money-grubbing," both sins of individualism in which one is concerned with oneself and one's own gain at the expense of others, are outlawed by the code. While Western morality has traditionally emphasized the individual, Soviet morality instead emphasizes society.

(4) A fourth peculiarity of Soviet morality, which makes it strikingly different from a Christian or Kantian morality, is that it is completely externalized. This means not only that its end is external, namely the benefit of society and not of self, but its virtues and even its concept of responsibility are in some sense external. The inner man is denied. Soviet man is his relation to society. This is what is considered real about him, and so this in fact is all, except biologically, that there is to him. The notion of a valuable solitude, of an inviolable interiority, is missing from Soviet morality and from the Soviet moral ideal. Responsibility itself is not something willfully assumed but something assigned as often to a collective as to an individual. The question of subjective guilt thus becomes more or less irrelevant. It makes little difference whether a person thinks he

has done right or wrong; what matters is whether he has done what he was supposed to do, where this is determined by his collective, or by the party. What is judged are external actions and their results, for these alone enter the sphere of morality.

In the "Moral Code of the Builder of Communism" there is no room for the notion that man is a law unto himself in the sense that he must do what he thinks is right even if this goes against what he is taught or against his society. Such a concept and such an ideal are considered individualistic and contrary to collectivist, socialist morality.

(5) A fifth characteristic of the Soviet moral code, and one which represents a basic difference between the Soviet and Western codes is that the respect for the person and for the individual, which is held by many of our deepest thinkers to form the basis of Western morality, is absent in the USSR. This is perhaps most obvious in the official attitude preached toward those who are not friends, comrades, brothers. While the tenth and twelfth principles call for friendship and fraternal solidarity among all workers and the peoples of the USSR, the eleventh principle demands "an uncompromising attitude to the enemies of communism, peace, and the freedom of nations." Part and parcel of communist humanism as taught in the schools is hatred of one's enemies.

This restricted humanism, joined with moral subservience to the party, results in a narrow moral provincialism. Though communist morality claims to be the development of an "all-human" morality, it can only be "all-human" when and if all mankind is communistic. It divides mankind into the communist and socialist builders of the society of the future and the objects of its morality on the one hand, and all others, those who are outside its pale, on the other. It is in fact a restricted morality for a part of a politically restricted world. It neglects what in our present world, made small by the speed of communication and the span of missiles, is common to all men. It ignores as well the common goal of human survival. It presents in sum a dogmatic, closed, self-assured morality which precludes rational inquiry by individual moral agents into what is good or right, and which demands obedience to a human but quasi-infallible authority which alone is able to determine what is right and what is wrong.

East European Variants

If Soviet ethics is monolithic and moralistic and if Soviet official morality is provincial and dogmatic, this does not mean that the situation is identical in the other East European countries. In the first place none of these has the long history of socialism which the Soviets have behind them. Having come to socialism only after World War II they are not as far along the road to communism, and they have more of the "remnants of capitalism" to contend with. Not yet faced with the immediate prospect of building communism, they do not yet have to worry about producing a new man with a new morality to people that society, as the Soviets do. They have not promulgated a new moral code and have made no assiduous attempts at inculcating the new communist morality, though communist moral norms are officially taught in at least some of the countries. Secondly, since in some of the East European countries more freedom of philosophical discussion is allowed than in the Soviet Union, different views and interpretations sometimes get a hearing.

The political dominance of the USSR is reflected also in moral philosophy in such countries as Czechoslovakia,[9] Rumania,[10] and East Germany[11] where we can speak, with respect to the ethical literature produced, of puppet presses. The few works turned out in this field are uniformly uninspiring second-hand Soviet Marxism-Leninism. This is not so, however, in Poland, Hungary, or Yugoslavia where interesting works in ethics have appeared.

In Poland the work of Ingarden is well known in the West, and M. Ossowska (who has attempted to develop a non-Marxist science of ethics) and N. Lubnicki (a positivist), among other non-Marxist philosophers, have contributed to the considerable Polish ethical literature since World War II. Most significant, however, are two Polish Marxists, one revisionist and the other, even by Soviet standards, quasi-orthodox. For they show that Marxist ethical theory need not go the way of the Soviets.

Leszek Kolakowski, the revisionist, takes his lead from the writings of the early Marx, leaving room for individual action, responsibility, and morality in a context of social and political development. He points up the need for moral principles in the present, and he refuses to sacrifice present morality on the altar of historical futurity. He thus insists on the necessity of morally evaluating contemporary socialism and the actions of present-day leaders and societies. The simple claim that an action supposedly leads to communism is insufficient to justify it, especially if it flies in the face of other moral principles.

The other, Adam Schaff, in *A Philosophy of Man* not only comes to grips with the Sartrean version of existentialism but also turns his attention to the meaning and value of life, individual responsibility and freedom, and the like. Contrary to Soviet practice he is opposed to moralizing and "to laying down moral standards from above." He holds, moreover, that "the demand for a Marxist ethics will not be realized until that ethics is developed in the spirit of a broadly understood philosophy of man."[12] As a program it points to an alternative Marxist approach to ethics and morality which, if developed, may well prove more philosophically interesting than the contemporary Soviet fare.

Hungary has followed the Soviet example of requiring the teaching of ethics in institutions of higher learning. There is much concern with the "degeneration of moral standards"; but little of philosophical value has emerged, with the exception of the already well-known works of Georg Lukács. Lukács' criticism of the ethics of Sartre, Simone de Beauvoir and Merleau-Ponty remains the best in the Marxist literature, his discussion of alienation the most profound since Marx. His notion of the individual's responsibility for history deserves more attention than Western philosophers have given it.

In Yugoslavia Marxist ethics holds sway, though there is diversity of Marxist interpretation. Djilas, the outspoken critic, has condemned communism for establishing a dual set of standards, one for the people, another for the ruling elite; and he categorically affirms that no special communist ethics can exist and that no special communist morality does exist.[13] But Mihailo

Marković seems better to represent current Yugoslav thought. In his article "Marxist Humanism and Ethics"[14] he goes far toward putting Marxist ethics in a contemporary Western philosophical idiom and toward making it relevant to problems discussed in the West.

What these non-Soviet East European philosophers offer the Western reader is a corrective to the Soviet model. For even from the few works referred to here it becomes clear that neither Marxist ethics nor communist morality need go the Soviet way. The Soviets have taken late Marx, Engels, and Lenin as their standard in ethics. The result is legalistic moralizing, and a morality that divides the present members of mankind into sheep and goats. The latter it excludes from its purview, even though it represents itself as the morality of all mankind in some mythical future time; the former it provides with a shepherd, the party, to serve as their conscience and to guide them down the road to Utopia. But there is another way, the humanistic way of the young Marx, around which not only the Kolakowskis and the Lukács's but also the Schaffs and the Marković can rally. The resulting ethics, it seems, will remain teleological and objectivist; but it need be neither so provincial nor so dogmatic as the present Soviet model. It can be used to evaluate critically not only capitalism but also socialism from a moral point of view. The morality it champions might be truly extended to all men if it seeks the free, all-round, harmonious development of all men in a just society, wherever and however this may be produced, instead of substituting for this aim its political name, communism.

The non-Soviet and especially the so-called revisionist developments of Marxist ethics have thus far been of more interest to Western philosophers than the Soviet. This is undoubtedly because Marxist ethics, which cannot be a reconstruction of Marx's supposed views on the subject, must be a critical rethinking inspired by his work. The dilemma of the Soviet moral philosopher lies in the fact that the critical and creative thinking which the problems of his discipline require is in great part precluded by the moralizing role which he has been assigned. It is a pity that he has not yet found a way to resolve his dilemma.

6

Dialectics
and Modern Science

■ The new Marxists we have looked at thus far are concerned
with history, society, man, humanism, and ethics. Among these
new Marxists we have found the non-Soviet writers in the avant-
garde; they are both more critical of socialist society and more
creative in their approach to Marxism than their Soviet counterparts. They go to the works of Marx for their inspiration,
and it is there, rather than in the writings of Engels or Lenin,
that they find their major themes.

In the realm of dialectics and dialectical materialism, the
most prolific writers are the Soviets, and it is in the Soviet Union
that we find the most interesting developments within the Marxist camp. This is not to say that the Soviet Marxist-Leninist
theory which emerges is truly creative. But in the area of dialectics Soviet writings are generally ahead of the rest of Eastern Europe, where the best minds have turned their attention
elsewhere.

The realm of dialectical materialism is in many ways more
dogmatized than the realms of historical materialism and the
theory of socialist development. There are several reasons for
this. In the humanistic fields the new Marxists were able to draw
on the writings of the young Marx to interpret and reinterpret
the writings of the later Marx and of Engels and Lenin. But
Marx left no treatment of dialectics as such which could serve
as a tool to support doctrinal changes. Secondly, the writings

of Marx on society were critical, and their critical edge could be turned against socialism as well as capitalism. In the theory of dialectics there is no similar critical edge. There is merely a polemical rejection of any non-Marxist theory, which is labeled either idealism or crude or mechanistic materialism. Thirdly, though the development of Soviet society from the start necessitated certain changes in the doctrine of historical materialism, for many years it had no such influence on the theory of dialectical materialism. By the 1940's dialectical materialism had become so embedded in Soviet Marxism that its practitioners used it even to challenge the findings of science.

Nonetheless in more recent times two factors have made for change in the doctrine of dialectical materialism. The first is the current attempt to make the terms and claims of the position more precise. The second, far more important, is the interrelation of the theory with particular sciences. In the crucial area of physics—so necessary for the development of nuclear power and modern technology—Soviet scientists initiated the battle against philosophical dogmatism. The liberation of scientific research from philosophical dogma, which started under Stalin, reached its culmination the decade after his death. Scientific developments have accordingly necessitated new interpretations of dialectical materialism and have limited its application.

Marx had described his method as dialectical. Though he acknowledged his debt to Hegel, he claimed that his own dialectical method "is not only different from the Hegelian, but its direct opposite." For while Hegel tied his dialectical method to his idealistic system, Marx interpreted dialectics from a materialistic viewpoint. He applied the dialectical method in his historical and economic writings, though he never wrote any specific treatise on dialectics. What precisely dialectics means in Marx's writings is not entirely clear, though it seems to mean at least that man is active and not passive in his knowing and doing, that he is dynamically interrelated with other men and nature, and that human reality is permeated with antagonisms which provide the motive force for change and development. His materialism consisted roughly of the beliefs that objects exist independently of man and his consciousness, that there are no purely spiritual entities such as God or angels, and that the only correct approach to practical social problems is to change their root cause, the economic conditions of society.

It was Engels who generalized the doctrine of dialectics and who applied it not only to human development and phenomena, but also to nature. And it is Engels' formulation of this general theory and its specific laws which Plekhanov dubbed "dialectical materialism." According to Engels, dialectics "is nothing more than the science of the general laws of motion and development of nature, human society, and thought." He specified three laws of dialectics which he took over from Hegel and for which he gave a variety of examples taken from nature, mathematics, history, and social development. The three laws are: 1) the law of the transition of quantity into quality and vice-versa; 2) the law of the interpenetration of opposites; and 3) the law of the negation of the negation. The first states that there are certain crucial (or nodal) points at which a quantitative addition produces a qualitative change. The second says that everything is in motion or development, and that its development stems from contradictions (antagonisms, oppositions) which are found within it. The third claims that, in general, development is progressive, and that from a conflict there arises a synthesis which negates what was negative in the antagonists, preserves what was positive, and elevates them into a new resultant. These laws, according to Engels, are exemplified on all levels of reality and in any and all of the sciences.

Engels' development of dialectics was taken over by Lenin who made certain reinterpretations of his own. He emphasized the interpenetration (or the unity and identity) of opposites, forged a Marxist theory of knowledge which was known as the "copy theory of knowledge," and attempted to apply dialectical materialism to science, defining and defending materialism against the Machian and neo-positivistic scientists in the beginning of the twentieth century.

The relation of Marxism to the sciences was still a much discussed question through the 1920's, as was the status of dialectics itself. But discussion was abruptly and officially terminated by a Stalinist decree on January 25, 1931. The period following was marked by the growth of dogmatism. Stalin dominated the entire intellectual scene and was correctly praised as the only innovator in Marxist-Leninist doctrine. No one else dared do anything but repeat or expostulate upon the words of their leader. The party became supreme in every realm, and dialectics was presented as a method to be used in the analysis of all phenomena and of social phenomena in particular.

The claims of omnicompetence on the part of the party and its leaders, however, collided with the facts of science during the latter portion of Stalin's reign. A first liberalization followed a speech by Stalin's spokesman A. A. Zhdanov in 1947; a second was the result of Stalin's writings on the linguistics controversy in 1950, in which he freed language from the base-superstructure dichotomy, claiming that it was not part of the superstructure and so could develop independently of superstructural considerations. The facts of science were acknowledged as having a similar position, as were mathematics and mathematical logic. Interpretations of science, however, still remained part of the superstructure and so tied to the doctrines of dialectical materialism. It is here that the disputes concerning science came to a head.

As the most general law of the development of nature, society, and thought, dialectical materialism does not imply any of the particular laws of any of the special disciplines. From the laws of dialectics one cannot deduce any particular law of physics or of biology or of any other science. This does not mean that it is completely neutral toward these sciences, but that the relation between them is not a deductive one.

The difficulties which the dialectical materialists have had with science came about primarily because some of them—often the leaders of the Soviet Union—proclaimed some particular scientific theory or position as true, not because of the scientific evidence for it, but because of its relation to dialectical materialism, claiming in some cases that the scientific theory in question could actually be deduced from it. This tendency has not been totally overcome; yet the best of the new Soviet Marxists seem clearly to have gone beyond such attempts.

The relation between dialectical materialism and the sciences is threefold. First, dialectical materialism is supposed to supply the general methodology for all the sciences. The methodology which it can supply however is very general and must be supplemented by the particular empirical methods of each particular science. The methodology consists primarily of general rules of procedure derived from the laws of dialectics. If there are contradictions in everything, if everything is in motion, if the process of development of everything is through negations and negations of the negations, then in each particular science these phenomena should be sought. But exactly how the phenomena are to be uncovered or handled thereafter must vary from discipline to discipline. If the dialectical method is not very helpful in specific research, it at least provides no insuperable handicaps; the laws as such need not impede a Soviet scientist and may direct his attention along certain lines, though we have no recorded evidence that it actually helps the scientific research of the Soviet scientists. Dialectical materialism has impeded the Soviet scientist only when certain unwarranted scientific conclusions drawn from it were dogmatically supported in the face of contrary scientific fact.

Secondly, dialectics is to serve as the guide for the interpretation of the facts of science. Each science must come up with its own finding. But once found, the interpretation of these facts is to be guided by the doctrines of dialectical materialism. When such interpretations are developed, the scientific discoveries are then said to validate or prove the correctness of the laws of dialectics. No interpretation which contradicts any of the laws of dialectics is acceptable to the party or to the Soviet Marxists. For the laws of dialectics are more certain to them than any particular interpretation of any particular science. While no particular law or theory is deducible from the laws of dialectics, no particular law or theory which contradicts them is said to be possible. In this way the dialectical laws serve as a negative check on the correctness of particular laws. The laws of dialectics are sufficiently flexible, however, to make this no great problem.

Lastly, there are certain general propositions which were enunciated by Engels and Lenin which have caused more difficulty for the Soviet scientist than they should have. One of these is the claim that the unity of the world consists in its materiality. Another is that space and time are objective and infinite. A third is that each level of organized matter has its own irreducible laws and its own movement. Each of these has caused some difficulty; nevertheless, each is still held, and all have been reconciled by reinterpretation in the light of the facts of science.

Though the Marxist position is materialistic, the materialism referred to is of a special kind, namely dialectical materialism. Marxism consequently rejects a simplistic approach to matter. It is anti-mechanistic and nonreductionist. It rejects the view that the higher forms of matter and the laws they follow can be reduced to the lower forms and their laws. There is a real and irreducible difference between animate and inanimate matter, and between conscious and non-conscious life. The former in each case developed from the latter but is not reducible to it. The explanation of how this is possible is primarily a philosophical problem and compatible with any facts of the evolution of life or consciousness which may be found by chemistry or biochemistry or any other discipline, for in the resulting life or consciousness there is a reality which differs from the inanimate and the unconscious, whatever its origin.

The Sciences

Soviet spokesmen are fond of pointing to Soviet triumphs in science and space technology as proof of the truth of dialectical materialism. Lenin in *Materialism and Empirio-Criticism* claimed that modern science was "giving birth to dialectical materialism," and S. T. Melykhin, a contemporary Soviet philosopher, similarly claims that "even those scientists who reject dialectics subjectively are forced spontaneously (due to the objective content of scientific concepts and theories) to follow dialectical laws and categories, since otherwise they cannot effectively work in the field of science."[1]

The truth of the matter, however, seems otherwise. Soviet scientists have made advances not because of but in spite of dialectical materialism. P. L. Kapitsa, a Soviet Academician and scientist, presents a more objective picture than many of his colleagues when he states: "Had our scientists back in the year 1954 paid attention to the philosophers . . . we may safely say that our conquest of space, of which we are so justly proud and for which the whole world respects us, could never have been made a reality."[2]

The details of the interference of the dialectical materialists and the party officials with acceptance of relativity theory and quantum mechanics in the Soviet Union have been sufficiently documented to need only a brief description here. The crux of the matter rested more on the interpretation of the two theories than on the facts; though because of what they considered idealistic interpretations, which contradicted the tenets of Marxism-Leninism, the philosophers were willing to ignore or deny the facts. In relativity theory some of the issues involved the apparent relativization of space and time, and the claim that the universe was finite. The philosophers, following Engels, claimed that space and time were objective and that the universe was infinite. Any admission of a finite universe, according to Engels, entailed the assumption of a creator or prime mover or God, which he rejected a priori. Consequently in arguing against the German philosopher Dühring, he argued for the infinity of the universe. Soviet philosophers felt similarly threatened by the implications of relativity theory and they chose to reject Einstein's theory, heaping abuse upon him in the process. Quantum mechanics also threatened the Soviet philosophers for it seemed to imply a denial of determinism and the objectivity of human knowledge, since both the position and momentum of a microparticle could not be known simultaneously. Engels and Lenin had defended determinism and the objectivity of human knowledge, and Soviet philosophers initially failed to see how they could admit the "uncertainty principle" without falling into idealism. Again they chose to ignore or deny the facts and attempted to carry their opinions over into the sciences.

Though they had been previously discussed, in the Soviet Union the theories of Einstein and Bohr came under attack by Soviet philosophers only after Zhdanov's speech in 1947. The battle raged in intense fashion especially during the early fifties. Einstein and the theory of an expanding universe were officially condemned and modern physics in general was attacked. But Einstein's theory was central to the building of the atomic bomb, and quantum mechanics to modern atomic physics, and in the end the physicists triumphed. By 1955 relativity theory was officially recognized and by 1958 indeterminism in quantum mechanics was similarly accepted.

The resolution, however, was not merely one of fact. Two things happened. First the philosophers learned—at least most of them did—that they could not deduce facts of nature from dialectical materialism and that the facts had to be accounted for, not ignored or dismissed. Secondly, they made serious—and partially successful—attempts to make the facts of modern science compatible with dialectical materialism. This has not been easy, and the question of the appropriate interpretation of both relativity and quantum mechanics is still a matter of discussion. But the discussion takes place on the proper philosophical level, often at joint conferences with physicists. The new Marxists deem it essential to produce Marxist interpretations of modern physics. They still claim confirmation for dialectical materialism from modern science. But they now seem ready to stretch the classical positions on determinism, matter, space and time, the objectivity of knowledge, and similar matters inherited from the works of Engels and Lenin, in order to accommodate the radically new findings of science.

Among the present Marxist interpretations of modern science we need only mention a few by way of example. The essential objectivity of the world and of matter is still defended, and if the infinity of the universe and the idea of an expanding universe is accepted it is offset by the claim first that such finitude does not necessitate a creator, and secondly, that nature is infinite at least in its structure (thus nominally preserving Engels' claim that nature is infinite). Space-time, it is claimed, is real and objective, even if it may be strictly correct to speak of the relativity of space and time in other respects. Similarly, the laws of nature are said to be objective, though they may pertain only to certain closed systems. The very existence of these closed systems—of classical mechanics, thermodynamics, electric and magnetic phenomena, quantum mechanics, the theory of elementary particles, and general relativity—is held to verify the claim of dialectical materialism that there are discontinuities or jumps in nature (the leap from quantity to quality). That particles display both corpuscular and undulatory behavior is taken as confirmation of the law of the interpenetration of opposites: nature is contradictory, and can therefore only be understood by a philosophy which admits contradictions and does not exclude them. The principle of indeterminacy is interpreted to show that Laplacian determinism, fatalism, and crude materialism are mistaken views, though it does not hinder the notion of determinism on the macroscopic level. Finally, the objectivity of knowledge remains part of the claim of dialectical materialism, though it is now emphasized that knowledge is dialectical, that it constantly increases, and that it cannot be said to be absolute or final.

The situation with biology is somewhat different from that with physics. The controversy in biology has centered around T. D. Lysenko, a Soviet agronomist, his defense of Michurinian biology, and the denial of Mendelian genetics. The classical theory of genetics in no way conflicted with any of the tenets of dialectical materialism; and neither Marx, Engels, nor Lenin had commited himself on specific questions of heredity, since, as we have seen, they held that man makes and transforms himself by his labor and by changing his society and social relations. In biology it was not any conflict with Marxist theory that was at issue. Rather it seems that Lysenko and his school were given official support by leaders of the communist party primarily for the promises of increased farm productivity which they offered, in contrast with the slower (though surer) methods proposed by the classical geneticists.

Lysenko and his school have had a roller-coaster career of ups and downs. Controversy between the Lysenkoites and the classical geneticists raged from 1936 until 1948, when Lysenko's position was declared the official line and criticism of it forbidden. Lysenko claimed that certain desired changes in offspring can be attained by environmental changes in the parents. He offered the hope of rapid transformations in both crop plants and animals according to the needs of the Soviet Union. His theories were followed, beginning with the agricultural crises of the 1930's. Programs based on his theories did not produce the results he had predicted and were often abandoned; but his theory remained. In 1953, after Stalin's death, classical geneticists were again briefly allowed to publish to a limited extent, though the Lysenko school still dominated. In 1950 Lysenko was removed from his post as head of the Lenin Academy of Agricultural Sciences, only to come back into favor less than two years later. Khrushchev re-enthroned Lysenko and forbade criticism of his position. Only after Khrushchev's downfall was Lysenko again deposed as chief of biology, though many important positions in the Soviet Union are still held by his followers.

The official endorsement of Lysenkoism seems to have stemmed mainly from its promise of more rapid improvement of Soviet agriculture and some actual successes, which caused its failures to be tolerated or ignored. The harm done was not so much to agriculture, which was still too primitive to benefit from sophisticated scientific techniques, as to genetic theory and research. In more recent years the failures have evidently been sufficiently important to make the Soviet leaders reconsider. Apparently, just as Soviet leaders once preferred to gamble on achieving effective practices by following Lysenko, they are now willing to gamble on the freer development of biological theory as the best way to achieve the desired increase in crop yields.

During these years of conflict, the philosophers who concerned themselves with Lysenkoism followed the party line. But they had no great influence, and dialectical materialism was never closely involved in the controversy.

Though cybernetics was initially rejected as bourgeois, it was never severely or extensively criticized as threatening dialectical materialism. When it was embraced it was embraced with enthusiasm because of the promise it held that by utilizing its techniques the Soviet Union could be more effectively led along some centrally guided path. The usefulness of computers and computer technology was soon realized by Soviet officials and

theoreticians, and despite early criticism cybernetics by 1955
was a respectable discipline with an ever-growing following.
Officially endorsed by the 1961 Program of the CPSU, it has
received official sanction in party statements since then. It is
being applied in economic control planning, industry, biology,
and medicine. Research institutes have sprung up, journals,
books, articles, and conferences on the topic abound. And all
this is the case despite the fact that Soviet computers are a
generation or two behind those in the United States, and their
shortage of working programs is acute.

The impact of cybernetics on Marxism in general has not
been significant. The possibility of control has renewed the hope
of some Marxists in the efficient building of a communist society
and in the eventual achievement of meaningful work for all,
with machines doing the drudgery. On the level of dialectical
materialism there were some who feared that cybernetics posed
a threat, since it provided a systems theory of the generality
of dialectical materialism itself, and one which might threaten
the laws of dialectics or the dichotomy between matter and
consciousness. Others saw in it a wave of the future, a set of
concepts which could be used to revivify dialectical materialism,
and they claimed that the whole theory would have to be re-
thought.[3] But in fact cybernetics thus far has neither posed a
serious threat to nor led to any major revisions of dialectical
materialism. For it seems to be philosophically neutral, carrying
with it no clear implications concerning matter and consciousness or the general laws of reality. In the United States, despite
initial enthusiasm, it has become recognized simply as an important tool; it seems likely that it will suffer the same fate in
the Soviet Union.

Can we draw any conclusions concerning dialectical materialism and the sciences and the effect the various controversies
have had on the Soviet Marxists? I think that we can. Though
there are still some old-guard Marxists who tend to dogmatize,
who feel threatened by any new theory in science, and who try
to deduce empirical and scientific claims from dialectical materialism with which to challenge the findings of science, it seems
they are a diminishing breed. The party has learned that it has

much to gain from science and its developments, and that science best serves the state if it is not directly interfered with. This is not to say that science is completely free from party control. But the party seems less given in recent years to dictate the content of science to scientists.

The Marxist philosophers have followed suit. From their battles with the physicists they seem to have learned two important lessons. One is that they cannot interpret and argue about science without knowing science. The other is that they cannot deduce scientific facts from dialectical materialism. Their task is still to interpret the findings of science and to reconcile them with the teachings of dialectical materialism. In this way they have become less dogmatic, and science seems to have a freer field of play than at any time since the 1930's. Soviet philosophers of science remain anti-idealistic, anti-bourgeois, and anti-positivistic, but the problems of interpretation with which they are dealing are genuine problems of the philosophy of science and are similar to the questions with which Western philosophers of science are grappling. The result is a lessening of dogmatism on scientific topics, a more receptive attitude to the findings of science and to scientists, and a more empirical and open approach to interpretation than in some other realms of Soviet Marxism.

Dialectics and Practice

Dialectical materialism is, together with historical materialism, the philosophical foundation of Marxism-Leninism. It is widely taught in the Soviet Union and helps make up the Marxist-Leninist world view, a framework into which all of knowledge and reality can be fit. But despite the lip-service paid by leaders of the party to dialectical materialism, it is far removed from practical politics and the building of communism. What the theoreticians and philosophers do within dialectical materialism makes little practical difference. It is for this reason that after the denunciation of Stalin Soviet philosophers could overnight switch from Stalin's presentation of dialectical materialism, which was in many ways anti-dialectical, back to Engels' version. They could not have made abrupt switches in the realm of historical materialism, even if they had wanted to, because the latter was tied to Soviet practices and social development in a way the former was not. Moreover, wherever dialectical materialism did impinge upon practical matters, the situation has been remedied, as in the case of relativity theory and quantum mechanics.

The disputes over formal logic ran a similar course. Lenin had identified logic, theory of knowledge, and dialectics. On this basis the official Soviet line for a long time was that the only true logic was dialectical logic, and that formal logic was static, metaphysical, bourgeois, and unnecessary. The first sign of a change in this position came in 1947. After Stalin's statements on linguistics, mathematical logic was freed from dogmatic control, and by the end of the 1950's a substantial literature in formal logic was developing in the Soviet Union despite the fact that a debate was still taking place concerning the status of formal logic and its relation to dialectical logic. Computers and computer theory, however, are tied to formal logical theory, and the necessity for formal logic was clear even if its theoretical position in the system of dialectical logic was cloudy. It was therefore allowed to develop, and the theoreticians were forced to find a place for it.

Perhaps the one exception to the general rule permitting practical considerations to take precedence over the theoretical considerations of dialectical materialism is found in psychology. The situation is complex in itself and has been complicated by the fact that Soviet psychology became intertwined with the theories of Sechenov and Pavlov, though neither was Marxist or dialectical in his approach. Their materialistic approach to man was attractive to the Marxists; but they both have strong tendencies toward reductionism (reducing mind and consciousness to matter and its laws), a position which is at odds with specific statements of Lenin and with the claims of dialectical materialism.

Lenin held that mind was not reducible to matter, though consciousness was a function of matter and its highest product. In this he followed closely in the footsteps of Engels, who divided the materialists from the idealists on the question of the primacy of matter. A materialist is one who claims that matter is primary, Engels asserted, while an idealist is one who claims that consciousness is primary. But if one were to reduce mind to matter or matter to mind, then the difference between idealism and materialism would be only in terminology. There would *ex hypothesi* be only one stuff, whether it was called "matter" or "mind."

Psychophysiology of a Pavlovian type has been allowed from the beginning of the Soviet period, but a general reductive psychology was taboo from the 1930's to 1950. Lenin's distinction between the brain and consciousness precluded a reduction to the former. Here dialectical materialistic theory dictated the correct position in psychology. In 1950, however, a conference on Pavlov's physiological teaching reopened the question of the relation of physiology to psychology and of the brain to consciousness. The connection of the two has been debated up until this day; though it is clear that both a dualism of mind and matter (or brain and consciousness) and an identity of the two are precluded by the doctrines of dialectical materialism.

Even here, however, where philosophy dictates to psychology, in the areas of applied psychology the psychologists have been allowed of late to go their own way and have been encouraged in their endeavors.

Industrial and social psychology are growing disciplines in the Soviet Union. But the Soviet approach to education and the rearing of the new man of Soviet society has in many ways been influenced more by the writings of A. S. Makarenko than by those of Pavlov. While Makarenko's teachings do not stem from dialectical materialism, they are close to the Marxist view of man as a collective being who is changed by his work and his social relations. Makarenko emphasizes the group and its educative power and illustrates how the group can bring pressure on the individual to educate him socially and to break him of his individualistic approach to life, his self-centeredness, and his asocial or anti-social behavior. The importance of the group in training and educating the individual, in molding opinion and in promoting social order has been of more practical significance and application in the Soviet Union than any of the more esoteric studies and experiments in psychology.

If the disputes between the Soviet dialecticians and the Soviet psychologists remain unresolved, it is undoubtedly in part because no practical consequences of the points at issue have been perceived. There is nonetheless one doctrine which the new Marxists are developing which deserves mention. Though it is found only embryonically in the writings of Marx, Engels, and Lenin, it may provide a bridge over the disputed issues. For Marx and Engels consciousness in man developed with need and together with language. But they state nothing about how consciousness developed from unconscious matter. Lenin simply claims that eventually science will be able to tell us exactly how it happened. Yet the question poses a problem which has not been faced head-on until recently in the Marxist literature. The answer which is being developed is that consciousness, which is the means by which man reflects the objective world outside himself, is in some analogous way an attribute of matter itself.[4] Reflection is thus said to be a general property of all states of matter, and it develops under appropriate conditions first into animal consciousness and then into human consciousness. The details of the position remain to be worked out; but the position reminds one of both Leibniz and Teilhard de Chardin, and it is a new emphasis of the new Marxists.

The Soviet Marxist theory of knowledge in general is still in a state of confusion and controversy, though few, if any, practical consequences follow from this philosophical muddle. The major difficulty stems from the Leninist sources within which the Soviet Marxists work. Lenin's *Materialism and Empirio-Criticism* presents a mechanistic, copy theory of knowledge in which man is akin to a mirror. His presentation in his *Philosophical Notebooks* is dialectical, with man an active knower; but he insists on the coincidence of dialectics, logic, and theory of knowledge, a claim which has still to be unraveled and which has generated a great deal of heat but little light. The only significant change in Soviet approaches to this problem consists in emphasizing the collective and historical aspects of knowledge.[5] In this view the problem no longer centers primarily on the individual consciousness of an individual knower, but knowledge is considered in its social dimension as well. The knowledge of mankind is not the result of any individual's making, nor is it possessed by any individual. Yet mankind knows the laws of physics, chemistry, the facts of history and geography, and so on, and it transmits this knowledge to the individual. It is obtained collectively, held collectively (and objectively in books and records), socially transmitted, and often used collectively, though consciousness is always individual. The approach is consistent with the Marxist view of man which we have seen and complements it. Whether it will or can be developed in any enlightening detail remains to be seen.

Dialectics and the New Marxists

What can we conclude from all this? The first conclusion is that there is a growing rift between dialectical and historical materialism. The dialecticians seem to be becoming less empirically oriented, the historical materialists, especially their humanistic wing, more so. While the latter are becoming more concerned with the development of socialism and the direction it is taking, the former have less and less pertinent contributions to make to the practical order. They have come up against science and found that dialectics makes no specific statements here, though it does propose a general, vague methodology and framework. They have retreated before the physicists and the logicians, felt threatened by the cyberneticians, and have allowed the psychologists to go their own way without challenge.

In their own domain, that of philosophy proper, the dialecticians are more closely tied to Engels and Lenin than to Marx, and more confined by dogma than their humanistically oriented East European Marxist confreres. In their approach they seem to be leaning more and more toward Hegelianism. Marxism from its inception has been torn between its materialism and the dialectics which it adapted from Hegel. The influence of

Lenin's *Philosophical Notebooks,* with all their Hegelian content, seems to be growing, and those interested in the questions of dialectical materialism are understandably turning toward Hegel and dialectics at the expense of materialism.

Dialectics remains a notable component of Marxism, and dialectical materialism, especially in the Soviet Union, has many defenders. But there can be no doubt that it plays less and less of a role in the actual functioning of society. It is less dogmatically applied to the sciences than formerly and yields no specific social or political practices. It is becoming more and more restricted to the philosophical domain where it properly belongs, and where it operates at such a high level of abstraction and with problems sufficiently recondite as to be outside the main stream of social life. Dialectical materialism is still taught in the schools, and popular books on it still fill the kiosks; some dialecticians still write for the masses. But the real work of the dialectical materialists, to the extent that they philosophize seriously, appears only in the specialized journals and in books of small editions.

7

Ideological Conflicts and Power Politics

■ In his eleventh Thesis on Feuerbach Marx announced that: "The philosophers have only interpreted the world in various ways; the point, however, is to change it." Marx's interests turned from the study of philosophy and philosophers to the study of political economy and to participation in and leadership of the workingmen's movement. But he never deserted theory.

If the point is to change the world, philosophers play their part in this enterprise not by giving up philosophy or theory, but by turning it to practical problems, by seeing clearly the true condition of man, by critically appraising it, by seeing what action must be taken, and by awakening the masses to all of this. For Marx the philosopher's job was to bring to the consciousness of the workers the recognition of their plight and of their need to revolt and seize the instruments of production. The world is not changed by abstract theories, but by people acting in the real world. Their action, however, can be guided by theory, and is most successful when that theory illuminates reality. According to Marx, theory and practical action were to be closely related, the former guiding the latter and the latter offering practical experience on the basis of which to correct the former. Theory and action ("praxis" or "practice") were to develop together—a doctrine which in Marxist

literature has come to be known as the interrelation of theory
and practice.

The doctrine is one which was followed and reiterated by
Lenin. For Lenin not only is "practice" the test of truth, but
the purpose of all thought is ultimately practice or action.
"Practice," he wrote in his *Philosophical Notebooks, "is higher
than (theoretical) knowledge."* There is reason to believe this
dictum is still held by the leaders of the Soviet Union.

Though Soviet leaders reiterate the need for interrelating
theory and practice, to what extent are they actually related
in the Soviet Union and the countries of Eastern Europe? We
have already answered this question in part in Chapter 1,
where we saw that Marxism or Marxism-Leninism was to provide a coherent world view for the people of socialist societies,
to justify the policies of the communist parties and rulers of
these societies, and to provide the ultimate end—communism—
toward which the socialist societies are striving. These general
functions should not be passed over lightly, for they are significant realities of socialist society, and without remembering
them some of the central differences between communist (or
socialist) and non-communist countries are lost.

Yet two remarks seem appropriate. The first is that theory
and practice in the Soviet Union, and in most of the other
socialist countries as well, have become separated, though not
divorced. Theory still provides the general framework within
which all official proceedings take place. The rulers and leaders of these countries still know their Marxism and undoubtedly believe in it. But the leaders are no longer the theoreticians. Marx supplied the basic theory and also took an active
role in the labor movement. Lenin led the October revolution
and was a revolutionary all of his life; yet he never forsook his
pursuit of theory. He wrote *Materialism and Empirio-criticism,*
a work dedicated to developing a Marxist theory of knowledge
suitable for handling the problems of the science of his day
and for refuting the idealists and Machists at the turn of the
century. In 1914 and 1915, while the World War raged in
Europe and the moment of revolution in Russia was fast ap-
proaching, he studied Hegel's *Science of Logic,* his *History of*

Philosophy and *Philosophy of History,* and Aristotle's *Meta-physics.* He did so not to while away the time but to sharpen his theoretical knowledge so he could better apply theory to practice.

With Stalin, who was not theoretically inclined, the rift between theory and practice began. The number of Stalin's theoretical writings is extremely small; but by his practical decisions the face and life of Russia were rapidly changed. Industry developed, and farms were collectivized. Many of the actions taken during his regime—the elimination of the kulaks as a class, the forced collectivization of the peasants, and so on—can be explained partly in terms of Marxist theory. But none of them can be directly deduced from it. The extent to which Marxist theory motivated any particular action of Stalin and of the Soviet Union is difficult to assess. The permanent changes which Stalin made to Marxist theory are found primarily in the realm of historical materialism, and they followed upon, rather than guided, certain practical decisions. Under Stalin the theory was developed *ex post facto* to justify actual practices. The doctrine of the active role of the superstructure is a case in point.

After 1922 Marxism moved into the Soviet schools and universities in full force. The Marxist professors became the theoreticians—teaching, writing, editing, and educating the masses in Marxism-Leninism. The party leaders became absorbed in the intricacies of ruling and leading a nation. Ideologists bridged the gap between theory and practice. Politicians or bureaucrats themselves, they issued directives concerning theoretical investigations and served as watchdogs over the theoreticians. Theory and practice were clearly no longer united as they had been in the persons of Marx and of Lenin.

Most of the developments which we find after Stalin's death and Khrushchev's speech in 1956 were in fact started under Stalin and can be found in embryo before his death in 1953. It was Stalin who encouraged discussion in 1947 and again in 1950, who allowed the sciences a certain amount of freedom—necessary for them to accomplish their military and technical tasks—and who removed the facts of science from the base-superstructure dichotomy; it was under Stalin that in 1946 psychology and logic were rehabilitated in the Soviet Union; and it was under Stalin that we witnessed a rupture in world communism with Tito's declaration of Yugoslavia's independence from the USSR, and the inauguration of national communism. It was also under Stalin that the Soviet Union started moving from a rule of terror to less violent means of social coercion and control. The continuity between the development both of theory and practice before 1956 and afterwards is thus greater than most contemporary Marxists admit.

Malenkov, Khrushchev, Kosygin, Brezhnev—none of them unite theory and practice the way Marx and Lenin did; all of them in this respect and in many others follow in Stalin's footsteps. The new Marxists of the Soviet Union and of Eastern Europe are the professors and the writers, not the politicians or their spokesmen. Some changes in theory—such as the claim that war between communist and capitalist nations is not inevitable, that peaceful coexistence is both possible and necessary—come from above and are dictated by practical necessity. A nuclear war, Khrushchev and his Soviet successors know, cannot help the Soviet Union in its quest for the good life. Their line is repeated by the philosophers, who are told by party directives to develop certain lines and defend certain actions of Soviet leaders. The more subtle changes in Marxist doctrine, the working out of a coherent and consistent position, the elaboration of previously undeveloped problems, and the like are regarded as the province of the philosophers and theoreticians, though they are also told to subordinate theory to practice, and to turn their attention to the pressing practical needs of Soviet society. Specific formulations of the laws of dialectics or of a workable theory of knowledge are no longer the concern of the leaders of society, though they were concerns of Lenin. The separation of theory and practice in contemporary Marxism exemplifies itself first, therefore, in the fact that the leaders of socialist society are no longer the theoreticians; and the theoreticians are no longer the leaders of society.

The interrelation of theory and practice is seen differently in the Soviet Union and in some other countries of Eastern Europe,

Yugoslavia in particular. In the Soviet Union there are some philosophers or theoreticians interested in their own particular scholarly endeavors, who proceed more or less freely in their own field without anyone worrying about the relation of their work to practical questions. As long as they do not disrupt the social order, or challenge the system, they are allowed to carry on their investigations. To be published their works must be within the Marxist or Marxist-Leninist framework. But a certain amount of theoretical dispute and difference of opinion is allowed in the technical or specialized journals and in the scholarly works, published in small numbers. For general consumption the party line is widely disseminated in popular works and texts, the intricacies of dispute glossed over or ignored. Even in questions dealing with practical matters, such as the laws of social development, or the question of the division of labor in socialism, disputes are tolerated if kept within bounds acceptable to the party leaders. Yet over-all, philosophy and theory are seen to be the handmaidens of practice, and theory is subservient to the regime and its fiat.

In Yugoslavia, though theory does not dictate practice, and though it is circumscribed to a large extent, Marxist philosophers—especially the "creative Marxists"—see the role of philosophy as one of criticism. They acknowledge that the leaders of the country are the leaders in politics and practical policy; but they claim for themselves the role of loyal critics whose function is to evaluate social or political practices from the viewpoint of Marxist humanism, and to pronounce judgment as they see fit. Complete freedom of criticism, as we know from arrests and imprisonments, is not tolerated, though much more criticism is allowed than in the Soviet Union. Moreover, the Yugoslavs are moving away from the Leninist notion of the party as the leader of society, and they are stressing the claim that social authority should be vested in the workers. This calls for a willing reduction in the party's power and its control over society. The party's function is to become one of guidance rather than control or coercion. The first steps have already been taken to implement these changes; if they are carried through, the communist party, at least in Yugoslavia, will con-

cern itself with theoretical direction instead of practical implementation. Presumably the philosophers will, as they have already, help define such terms as "social self-government" which
is used to describe Yugoslav society, and they will contribute
more directly to the party's directive work than is the case
in the Soviet Union. Presumably they will also continue to
serve as loyal critics and exponents of Marxist humanism.

It must be admitted, however, that on the level of specific
decisions and attempts to resolve particular problems, the Marxist framework is too diffuse, too ambiguous, too vague and
broad, and too open to different interpretations to enable anyone to deduce from it any specific set of actions. It provides the
general goal of communism and specifies some particular means,
namely the abolition of classes and of the private ownership
of the means of production. But it does not say how these are
to be accomplished. Many of the practices which were defended
as necessary and in accordance with Marxist theory have since
been said to violate that theory. Political analysts have often
remarked that on the basis of Marxist theory one cannot predict how the Soviet government will react to any particular
international event. The Soviet decision to withdraw its missiles
from Cuba was not deducible from Marxist theory, nor is their
stand on any particular military or political question. What
their stand probably will be can be guessed on the basis of
their past actions. But this is often referable to pragmatic self-
interest or to power politics, and not to Marxist doctrine. Those
who wish to be able to deduce particular actions from Marxist
doctrine will try in vain; for they are not deducible. General
ends are stated and given by the doctrine; but the particular
means of attaining them are not. Nor have any Marxists claimed
they were.

It is true that one cannot deduce what a certain individual
or nation will do in a given situation simply from one's knowledge of beliefs or doctrine. But to think one could, would be
to ascribe to the doctrine more than any of its adherents claim
for it. One could not deduce what Kennedy would do, simply
because he was Catholic and Democratic rather than Protestant

and Republican. Yet this does not mean that beliefs do not form part of the way individuals view problems and situations.

That a great many different and seemingly contradictory actions are compatible with Marxism and with any other general set of beliefs should be sufficiently obvious to cause little comment, though strangely it provokes a great deal. What seems more to the point, however, is that many of the doctrines of Marxism, such as the belief that the three laws of dialectics operate on all levels of reality, do not carry with them any particular, definite course of action. This belief may make one look for contradictions in a situation, for alternative ways of action, for the possible reactions, or it may make one more tolerant of existing contradictions. But one can also take all this into account without belief in the laws of dialectics. On the practical level, every action is compatible with these laws, since if any action is performed it conforms by definition to the laws. The dialectical approach may color the way one evaluates or explains or justifies an action *post hoc*. It does not lead to any particular action *ante hoc*. It is this aspect of the relation of Marxist theory to communist practice which most commentators have in mind when they claim that the actions of the Soviet Union can be explained and analyzed in terms of practical self-interest and power politics, without recourse to Marxist theory. In any particular international event this is correct, providing always that one keeps in mind the fact that the theory supplies the end for which all communist actions must ostensibly strive, namely the achievement of communism.

That particular actions cannot be deduced from Marxism and that in many cases an indefinite number of actions are compatible with Marxist doctrine, however, is a doctrine which cuts two ways. If one cannot deduce a particular action on the basis of it, neither can one insist that a particular political system follows from it. This aspect of the question is stressed not by the Western critics but by the new Marxists who are anxious to dissociate themselves from the negative aspects of Stalin's reign and who claim that the abuses perpetrated in the Soviet Union were not a result of Marxist doctrine but took place in spite of it. They claim that neither totalitarianism nor the use of terror either stem from or are demanded or condoned by Marxism. In the name of Marxist humanism they reject both, though others can cite texts in support of both, providing they are in some sense necessary.

Totalitarianism provides a model which Western analysts have used with profit to describe the Soviet Union, especially under Stalin. Totalitarianism is one possible application or interpretation of Marxism. Lenin did in fact so interpret Marx, adding the doctrine of *partiinost'*, according to which the party and its leaders become the vanguard of the proletariat, and the leaders and guardians of all aspects of life. The totalitarian model has been found, however, to have shortcomings in describing Soviet reality. Authoritarian, though not totalitarian, models have been suggested and used. Simple industrial models are also revealing. There is no doubt that many aspects of Soviet life reflect the authoritarian—and paternalistic—approach of the party, as well as many of the characteristics of any industrial society. But neither authoritarianism nor industrialization are the direct results of following Marxist doctrines, and there are many intervening connective links. To speak about either authoritarianism or about industrialization in the Soviet Union may be enlightening in many ways, but it throws little light on what is Marxist about Soviet society. The same is true *mutatis mutandis* about the other countries of Eastern Europe.

What is distinctively Marxist is somewhat nebulous. For Marxism is never found pure and unadulterated. The emphasis on collectivism results, as we have seen, from one interpretation of the Marxist notion of man. This has ramifications in the way Soviet society is organized. The abhorrence of private ownership of the means of production is Marxist, though smugness about state ownership is not. The goal of communism is taken from Marx and informs the internal structure of Soviet society and of priority planning. Marxism brings with it a great many values and value judgments, some of them compatible with any industrial society, some of them antagonistic to certain aspects of industrialism as found in capitalist countries. These values were carried over into Russia and Eastern Europe and superimposed upon peoples who had differing value systems—agricultural or Christian or Orthodox, individualistic or semi-feudal. Each country has assimilated some of the Marxist values, and has been unwilling to accept others.

In many ways, however, the development of the Soviet Union since World War II shows more continuity than change in the periods after Stalin and after Khrushchev. Each of the leaders had his own peculiar methods and idiosyncrasies. But there has been no more radical shift in policies, for instance, than there has been in the United States, despite changes in administrations since World War II. Each country is too vast, too dynamic in its development, and too varied to be changed radically by any one individual.

The new Marxism which has emerged and is emerging from the Soviet Union and Eastern Europe is not the result of either the death or direction of any individual or small group. Rather it represents and coincides with the growing industrialization, the growing literacy and level of education, the growing amount of leisure time, the growing number and variety of goods and services available in these countries. The Marxist doctrine of the determination of the superstructure by the base is an oversimplification. But it has more than a kernel of truth in it; and the new Marxism can and should be understood in relation to the economic and social development of the Soviet Union and Eastern Europe.

Similarities and Differences in Eastern Europe

World communism is no longer a monolithic worldwide movement. If Moscow was ever the Third Rome, there is now good reason to believe there may well be a fourth. Its hegemony has been challenged, and commentators for some years have been speaking of polycentrism within the communist bloc. For a long time the Soviet Union was the only country in which a successful revolution had been achieved in the name of Marx, and the Soviet Union dominated the world communist movement.

The Soviet Union extended communism to the governments of much of Eastern Europe and backed up their communist regimes by the force of its arms. It dominated these countries to an extent which justified calling them satellites. But in one country, Yugoslavia, communism had been won not from the outside, but from within. Though Yugoslav communism was initially modeled on the Soviet pattern and though Yugoslavia was largely subservient to the Soviet Union, it was not completely so. This led first to a denunciation and boycott of the Tito regime, and then to a break between Yugoslavia and the Soviet Union with Yugoslavia successfully defending its independence and creating a type of national communism. A third center emerged in China, where Chinese revolutionaries had also won their own battle and established their own communist regime in 1949. Initially they too had followed the Soviet lead in international affairs. But by 1958 tension between the two countries was growing. The dispute broke into the open in 1960 and the rift has grown since then. Though the Sino-Soviet dispute has often been called an ideological one it is both much more and considerably less than that. It is less because both parties still recognize the authority of Marx and Lenin, and both are striving toward the same end of world communism. They differ on means, and the dispute really centers on the question of leadership of the world communist movement.

In the realm of doctrine two points seem to be at the center of the Sino-Soviet dispute, both of them traceable to Stalin, though made explicit by Khrushchev. The first claims that war between the communist and capitalist countries is no longer inevitable for the triumph of communism. The second, similar to the first, is that violent revolution is no longer inevitable for the triumph of communism. Both doctrines represent the Soviet recognition that in a nuclear age any all-out war, and any confrontation of nuclear powers on the opposite sides of a revolution could trigger a nuclear war which would be disastrous to both sides. This position China rejects, at least in theory, calling the United States a paper tiger. Despite their supposed differences on these issues, however, the actions of the Soviet Union and China have not been noticeably in accord with their statements. China has cautiously avoided any confrontation with the United States, even to the extent of keeping its hands off Formosa and the islands closer to its own shore. And the Soviet Union has continued to support revolutions as it sees fit, whether they be in Cuba or Viet Nam.

The dispute between China and the USSR is over leadership and does not depend primarily on personalities, either of Stalin or of Khrushchev or of Mao. Other differences between the two countries are also present: boundary disputes, long-term national enmity, the question of race, and so on.

The upshot of the dispute has been maneuvering on the part of both China and the Soviet Union for the allegiance of the communist parties throughout the world. This maneuvering has in turn allowed many of the countries of Eastern Europe room for their own maneuvering, as they seek concessions from the Soviet Union in payment for their support.

There are many sources of unity between the Soviet Union and Eastern Europe (with the exception of Albania which is firmly in the Chinese camp, and Yugoslavia, which is quasi-independent). Ideology is one important cohesive factor. The common allegiance to Marxism and the achievement of communism provides the basis for a similarity of outlook and for united action. More tangible links arise from the history of the development of these countries and the Soviet Union after World War II. Military, economic, and political ties bind Eastern Europe to the Soviet Union more strongly than to any other country. On the international level the governments of these countries follow the lead of the Soviet Union as undeviatingly as they did during Stalin's lifetime. On the domestic level this is not always the case.

The principal divisive agent in the communist bloc is without doubt nationalism, a trait which forms a stumbling bloc for Marxism and world communism. If the Soviet Union set the example by equating what was good for itself with what was good for the communist movement, the other countries of Eastern Europe have learned the lesson well. The Hungarian and Polish uprisings can be read more clearly as a protest against Soviet domination than as a protest against Marxism or communism. Differences of nationality, religion, language, history, and geography are all tied in with the question of nationalism and all serve as divisive forces within the communist movement.

The leaders of the Soviet Union have come to acknowledge the break-up of monolithic unity. Though they still exercise leadership in Eastern Europe, they have become tolerant of the expression of nationalistic interests on the domestic level, and of divergencies of opinion on the level of theory. Ideological differences apparently cause them little concern as long as on practical matters their leadership is acknowledged, their interests protected, and their influence accepted.

The Significance of the New Marxism

In its Soviet version the new Marxism is neither startling nor radically different from the Marxism prevailing during the later period of Stalin's life. Its tone is more subdued, its bombast is less extravagant, its criticism of opponents is somewhat more restrained, and its language is less harsh, though there still remain exceptions. If it has become somewhat more filled with controversy than before, it still presents a fairly uniform front and its spokesmen claim agreement on many issues and predict agreement on those points presently in dispute. Marxist theoreticians are not one of the more liberal or progressive groups in the Soviet Union. Soviet philosophers and ideologists do not protest against censorship, party control, or stifling restrictions the way the Soviet poets, writers, and artists do. We have yet to have any significant Soviet philosophical work smuggled out of the Soviet Union and published abroad, as is the case with literary works.

Yet despite all this there have been, as we have seen, some changes. Soviet philosophers are less prone to deduce empirical facts from their world view than previously, and they are more ready to accept the facts of science and to interpret them rather than deny them. In the realm of historical materialism too, the Soviet theoreticians are turning more and more to empirical data—to sociology, psychology, and economics—upon which to base their generalizations. But all too often they still refuse to accept any account of the bourgeois or capitalist or non-communist world except those that fit their own preconceived ideas and schemes.

In the realm of politics, Soviet theory remains subordinate to Soviet national and party demands. It serves not so much to mold policy as to justify and explain it.

On the whole the new Soviet Marxism is remaining essentially in its Marxist-Leninist mold, though within that mold its practitioners are attempting to render it more consistent, intellectually sophisticated and palatable than hitherto. They are consequently not undermining it, but strengthening it, though in the process some changes are necessarily being introduced, some new doctrines suggested, and some old ones revised or reinterpreted.

The new Marxism in some of the rest of Eastern Europe is by contrast refreshingly diverse. It seeks dialogue with representatives of other positions, be it with existentialists, positivists, or Christian humanists. It is turning to new problems and is throwing off many of the accretions of Lenin and Stalin in favor of a twentieth-century Marxism. It is in many ways still dogmatic, but no more so than many other philosophical schools. In countries like Yugoslavia it is the Marxists who are in the vanguard of social protest and who vocally demand reform, the lessening of party domination, and the development of true democracy.

What we learn from comparing the development in the new Marxism as a whole in both the Soviet Union and the countries of Eastern Europe is that Marxism is still very much alive. Its variety of expression moreover is convincing proof that Marxism need not go the way of Lenin and Stalin and that communism need not go the way of Stalinist Russia.

Marxism contains within it untapped sources which are not antithetical to other developments in modern thought. If Eastern Europe is any indication of its vitality, it seems to develop more fruitfully when crossed with other trends, when its practitioners sharpen their analytical tools and widen their existential horizons. The availability of Western philosophical literature varies from country to country. In Yugoslavia it is relatively accessible; in the Soviet Union even many of the

classics of modern philosophy are unavailable. In Czechoslovakia Christian-Marxist discussions have taken place similar to
those in France and Italy; the Soviet theoreticians have difficulty talking with the Marxists of Yugoslavia and are reluctant
to admit that the latter are Marxist at all if they are not
Marxist-Leninists.

Polycentrism has arisen within the communist bloc. Its
power centers differ from its creative centers of theoretical
activity, but the doctrine of communism still remains a common bond among them all. The first test of the viability of
the new Marxism may well take place in Yugoslavia if the
party there gradually relinquishes its power, as it has claimed
it would. Critical and loyal Yugoslav Marxists will fall in with
the party's desire to be the guide and not the director of social development. But whether Marxist ideology, Marxist humanism, and the Marxist scheme of values will hold the allegiance of the workers and common people in their attempt at
self-government or whether it will be replaced by some other
goal or ideology still remains an open question. The new Marxists are presently the intellectuals, the theoreticians, or the
party spokesmen. Though their doctrines are more alive and
creative than the moribund Marxism-Leninism of the Stalin
period at its worse, there is still no way to tell if it has cap-
tured the mind or spirit of any significant portion of the people.

If Marxism has been imposed in communist countries by
force, it does not necessarily mean that it will continue only
as long as it is backed up by force. For the more these societies are built on the principles of socialism or communism,
the more likely it is that Marxism will continue to live. If
some East European countries and peoples have arisen against
foreign domination, they have not clearly arisen against socialism. There seems ample reason to believe both that most
of the people of socialistic countries do not want capitalism
and that they are loyal to their national leaders. That they do
want reforms and changes is compatible with Marxist doctrine,
and in fact most of their demands can be made in the name
of Marxism. Marxism should not therefore be equated either
with Stalin or with the Soviet Union, nor with the Marxism-

Leninism of Stalin or the Soviet Union. By implication this also means that the Marxism-Leninism of the Soviet Union itself may some day follow the more liberal lines of other countries and may develop creatively, in ways it is impossible to predict.

One strong indication of the vitality of the new Marxism is the interest in it of an increasing number of Western philosophers and intellectuals. There was scarcely any interest in the Marxism-Leninism of the Soviet Union during Stalin's reign, not because the works were in Russian but because they were intrinsically uninteresting—dogmatic, repetitious, and offering no new insights, problems, arguments, or creative thought. By contrast there is today growing interest in the Marxists of Yugoslavia, and, in some cases, of Poland, Czechoslovakia, and Hungary. Their works are translated into English, French, German and other languages not by their own translators but by Western translators; their contributions are increasingly sought by and appear in Western philosophical journals, in anthologies, and in symposia. Conferences and "dialogues" have arisen. In some quarters the writings of a Kosík or of a Petrović generate an interest and response that no Soviet philosopher has yet succeeded in generating. As Marxism opens itself to other questions than those treated by Marx and Engels, it becomes more and more relevant to questions being studied by others with different views, and cross-pollination between and among different schools of thought becomes possible and desirable. The rise of the new Marxism is tied to the liberalization of thought in those countries where it has taken place, and it is significant as a sign of such liberalization and as an indication that there are ideas and values present in Marxism which make it alive and attractive.

For Marx and many of his followers Marxist doctrine was both true and scientific. At least many of its truths are now held to be only "relatively true," i.e. to have accurately portrayed the conditions of his time or to contain a kernel of truth which has to be developed, clarified, and applied in different ways in different contexts. The claim that Marxism is "scientific" is still made by the Soviet Marxists, though the meaning of "scientific" seems much closer to the English mean-

ing of "true" or "valid knowledge" than to what we usually
mean by "science." The doctrines of Marxism, new or old, are
not scientific empirical statements, and any attempt to see them
or evaluate them as such is beside the point. Of course, if a
Marxist, Soviet or otherwise, makes such truth-claims, then his
assertions can be evaluated. But for the most part among thinking Marxists, Marxism is not said to be an empirical discipline,
verifiable by empirical means in the same way that relativity
theory or genetic theory are. We have seen that the Soviet
confrontation with empirical science has forced a healthy with-
drawal from pretensions of this sort.

How then are we to consider Marxism? I suggest looking at
it briefly in its function as a philosophical enterprise, as a
nonrepresentational myth, and as an ideology.

In the Anglo-American world, philosophy is commonly held
to be concerned primarily with analysis. Its function is to
analyze concepts, arguments, and presuppositions. It is an
activity rather than a set of propositions or beliefs. One judges
it, therefore, not by the extent to which it can be verified—
since there is no proper content to verify; rather one evaluates the validity of the arguments put forth or the clarity with
which the concepts are elucidated. Among the new Marxists,
there are some who are carrying on the analytic activity of
philosophy within the Marxist framework. They are attempting
to clarify concepts and to present and evaluate arguments. But
their number is small and the new Marxists are not known or
noteworthy for their philosophical analysis.

A second traditional function of philosophy has been called
synthesis, or the attempt to unify man's experience into a coherent whole. Marxists often claim that their system is a synthesis of the sciences, based on them and supported by their
findings. But this is quite clearly not the case, for as we have
seen the new Marxist approach is to attempt to interpret the
findings of science, rather than to build upon them. What
Marxism presents is a scheme, loosely knit, somewhat ambiguous and often vague, into which various aspects of reality from
history to science, from thought to politics, are to be fitted and
in terms of which they are to be described. It offers a vague

set of terms or categories which allow for descriptions of a wide variety of phenomena. It achieves its generality precisely by its vagueness. It might loosely be called a world view, and is so identified by its Marxist supporters.

Within this framework, moreover, we can justify a number of myths. Levi-Strauss claims that the function of a myth is to render intellectually and socially tolerable the order of society as experienced. In a primitive society the myths employed are representational, and often involve a hero or story. Modern myths, however, are most often nonrepresentational and do not necessarily involve any hero or story line. They are conceptual, in keeping with the greater conceptualization of modern scientific thinking, and are compatible with the findings of science, at least so long as they retain their force and usefulness. As myths they necessarily go beyond what constitutes knowledge for the period in which they are found. They therefore constitute not knowledge but beliefs, and they function as belief systems.

This notion of modern, non-representational myths should not be restricted to Marxism. Most systems which present themselves as explanations or justifications of the social order and of man's experience as a whole fall into the same category. One can think of fascism as a myth, the myth of a master race with a certain destiny. One can similarly approach the doctrine of laissez-faire as a myth operated in the realm of politics and economics. The claim that all men are created equal and endowed by their Creator with inalienable rights can also be considered as a myth in that it goes beyond any establishable facts to state beliefs which justify certain social structures.

These modern myths may be of at least three main types. If they propose a total, all-embracing scheme of the world, which purports to be the one and only proper description or way of conceiving the world, it has traditionally been called metaphysics; here we have a totalizing myth, which explains the world, where by "explanation" we mean the connecting together of concepts into an intelligible whole. A second type is teleological. It goes beyond present experience, extrapolating from it and presenting the direction of the world's development. Its function is also explanatory or justificatory, for it attempts to make sense out of the present and past in terms of what it conceives the future will be. It is not a prediction, but a belief, and may be concerned with projecting the future destiny of the world as a whole or of smaller units within the whole. A third type is a moral myth. This presents a certain set or scheme of values, be they moral, social, esthetic, or other. The value scheme is presented as objective, and so is used to evaluate (justify or condemn, as the case may be) given institutions, practices, or actions.

Now with all of these myths we cannot accurately speak of verifying them or of their being true or false. They are, however, susceptible to evaluation, though the evaluation concerns their adequacy to the function they are to perform, rather than to their supposed truth-value.

To the extent that they are believed, they in fact serve to justify or give meaning or sense to the activity of the individual or group which believes them. They can serve as an impetus to action and can supply a sense to life. When they fail to do so, however, we can speak of the loss of belief or disillusionment; and they are then often replaced by other beliefs or myths. Some such beliefs are necessary because man does not know enough about the world in which he lives to operate only on the basis of scientific knowledge, and values by their very structure are not directly and unambiguously derivable from facts without some sort of initial value judgment or set of beliefs. Myths can be made more believable and patched up, developed, made more rational, and so on. They may also be replaced by some other myth or myths which are intrinsically more believable. Myths are partial renderings of reality, partial accounts or justifications which are presented as complete explanations or justifications. When what has been unaccounted for demands recognition, they must be repaired or replaced.

If we view belief systems in this way, we see that most of them have not been disproven; they have simply proven inadequate to the needs of those who held them and have been more and more ignored. This is true of many of the great systems of philosophy and of many social theories, from the divine right of kings to the myth of rugged individualism. As life and society changed, the values and justifications these theories provided were no longer pertinent or adequate.

There is one further aspect of these myths which we should mention. As myths they may be the result of the thinking of a single individual or of many; they may be formed all at once or develop gradually over many years and generations; they may be held by a single individual or by many. We can view an ideology as being a myth or group of myths either commonly held by a large segment of a society or as officially promulgated by the leaders of that society. Ideologies are thus open to the same kinds of development and replacement as myths, though they operate on a broader level and are used to justify social actions or institutions to or by the members of a society.

If we now view Marxism within this context, we can see that it in fact offers a totalizing myth in the doctrine of dialectical materialism; a teleological myth in the doctrine of the eventual triumph of communism, toward which society is tending; and a moral myth or scheme of values in terms of which certain actions and institutions are justified, and societies judged. It is certainly an ideology at least to the extent that it is promulgated and used by the leaders of ruling communist parties to justify their actions. It may also be believed by a significant number of people within the Soviet Union and the countries of Eastern Europe. It is almost certain that significant portions of these people believe certain aspects of these myths. They do not all stand or fall together. One can certainly believe that communism contains certain values worth working or fighting for, without believing that communism is inevitable or that all of history or all of nature operates according to the laws of dialectics. Part of the strength of Marxism as an ideology is precisely that it can be taken piecemeal by the people of a society, though its purist defenders would probably deny this.

What of the new Marxism? It seems clear that classical Marxism, as a social myth, proved inadequate at certain crucial stages in its development. Lenin saw the need to revise it to fit the Russian situation so it could become believable and applicable in that country. Stalin late in his reign must have also realized that in order to mobilize the Soviet people to work toward building communism the Marxist myths had to be revitalized, made more relevant to the needs of the people, and developed. The new Marxists seem similarly conscious of this need. With increased industrialization and rising standards of living the Marxist myth which appealed to revolutionary ascetics no longer sufficed for a population eager for more comforts and rewards for devoted labor. The rise of the new humanistic Marxists can be seen as a response to the need for a new dimension which had been ignored during the Stalinist era. Even the new Soviet Marxist approach to science and dialectics can be seen as a response to the need for making the myth more rational, more coherent, and more believable and acceptable to a people who were becoming better and better educated and more critical in their approach to the official ideology, which they were questioning more and more. The Marxist myth was too simple. The new Marxists attempt to account for aspects of reality which Marx squeezed into a system of dichotomies. There are not only two classes, but many. Good and bad are not simply equatable with proletariat and bourgeoisie respectively. The superstructure influences the base as well as the base the superstructure. Individuals as well as masses act in history and should accept responsibility for it. And so on. The intellectuals still have not been satisfied and many parts of the myth are no longer adequate for them. But despite their rejection of many parts of it, they too seem to accept many of the positive values of brotherhood, helpfulness, peace, social justice, and so on which the myth propounds and which the governmental leaders all too often violate in practice. From this point of view the myth is more attractive than the reality, and some reject their present social institutions or regimes precisely because they do believe the myths and espouse the values contained therein.

The new Marxists thus serve a paradoxical function. To the extent that they are believers in the myths of Marxism they attempt to strengthen them, rethink them, make them more acceptable to themselves and to others, and more pertinent to the realities in which they find themselves. To this extent they strengthen and uphold the existing social order and the communist parties in power. This is the function desired by the leaders of the party and one which promotes the careful control of philosophy in the Soviet Union. But to the extent that the new Marxists make their myths more rational and believable, more noble and pertinent, they also tend to raise the expectations of the people higher. The critical function of the creative Marxists in Yugoslavia is a clear example of this, though even in the Soviet Union this aspect of the new Marxism should not be ignored. To the extent that they do make the myths stronger, more coherent, more believable, more pertinent, they force the rulers to function in terms of the higher ideals, and to change society more rapidly in accordance with their own proclaimed beliefs and values. This is the danger of a freely developing and responsive ideology. It is a danger of which the leaders of the Soviet Union seem clearly conscious, since they impose ideological restrictions whenever the theoreticians and intellectuals start to run too far ahead of what the leaders see as possible. The see-sawing of Soviet policy with respect to the control of intellectuals and of theory seems to bear this out. The same is true in Czechoslovakia, Poland, Hungary, and to some extent Yugoslavia.

In order to make the ideology palatable it must be changed; but changes in values and justifications often lead to popular expectations which political leaders feel they cannot provide or are unwilling to provide. In either case they are faced with an ideological dilemma. Either the ideology is safe, but less and less believed; or it becomes pertinent to real life, but a threat to the power and control of the leaders by the unfulfillable demands which it creates in the people.

The new Marxists have shown that Marxism is still alive and that it can be made more pertinent than it had been under Stalin. From the variety of the Marxisms which are emerging it is also clear that it would be foolhardy to try to predict what the new Marxism may eventually become. It is also clear that when compared to the Stalinist version of Marxism-Leninism, it has nowhere to go but up, and that in changing and developing it has nothing to lose but its dogmatic chains. The new Marxism will get more interesting, but most East European regimes cannot afford to let it get too interesting too fast.

Notes

NOTES TO CHAPTER 1

1   Karl Marx and Frederick Engels, *Selected Correspondence,* Moscow: Foreign Languages Publishing House, p. 496.
2   *Pod znamenem marksizma,* 1922, No. 3, p. 9.
3   Joseph Stalin, *Works,* Moscow: Foreign Languages Publishing House, 1953, vol. 6, p. 92.
4   *The New York Times,* June 26, 1967, p. 19.
5   E. V. Il'enkov, "From the Marxist-Leninist Point of View," *Marx and the Western World,* ed. Nicholas Lobkowicz, Notre Dame: University of Notre Dame Press, 1967, p. 401.

NOTES TO CHAPTER 2

1 See, for example, A. E. Furman, "O predmete istoricheskogo materializma," *Filosofskie nauki*, 1965, 6, pp. 85–90; M. S. Dzhunusov, "O vzaimosviazi osnovnykh poniatii istoricheskogo materializma," *Voprosy filosofii*, 1965, 7, pp. 144–146; M. Kammari, "Nekotorye voprosy teorii bazisa i nadstroiki," *Kommunist*, 1956, 10, pp. 42–58; V. P. Tugarinov, "O kategoriiakh 'obshchestvennoe bytie' i 'obshchestvennoe soznanie,'" *Voprosy filosofii*, 1958, 1, pp. 15–26.

2 Karl Marx, *Capital*, Moscow: Foreign Languages Publishing House, 1959, p. 8.

3 *Ibid.*, p. 10.

4 On this point, see F. V. Konstantinov and V. Zh. Kelle, "Istoricheskii materializm—marksistskaia sotsiologiia," *Kommunist*, 1965, 1, p. 12; P. N. Fedoseev, "Dialektika razvitiia sotsializma," *Kommunist*, 1965, 14, p. 22; V. N. Cherkovets, "Osoznatel'nom ispol'zovanii ekonomicheskikh zakonov v sotsialisticheskom obshchestve," *Voprosy filosofii*, 1964, 7, pp. 3–13; A. Spirkin, *Kurs marksistskoi filosofii*, Moskva: Izdatel'stvo "Mysl'," 1966, p. 293.

5 A. F. Shishkin, "Problema sotsial'nogo determinizma i morali v rabotakh V. I. Lenina," *Voprosy filosofii*, 1967, 4, pp. 22–23.

6 *Nekotorye aktual'nye voprosy marksistsko-leninskoi teorii*, Moskva: Izdatel'stvo "Mysl'," 1966, p. 3.

7 *Pravda*, Jan. 14, 1967, as quoted in *Communist Affairs*, Jan.–Feb. 1967, p. 22.

8 For a fuller discussion of this see Richard T. De George, *Patterns of Soviet Thought*, Ann Arbor: Michigan University Press, 1966, pp. 184–201.

9 *Praxis*, 1967, 1, p. 62.

10 *Ibid.*, p. 12.

11 *Praxis*, 1967, 2, pp. 179–180.

12 *Praxis*, 1967, 1, p. 64.

13 Part II, section VII.

14 *Praxis*, 1965, 2/3, p. 178.

15 *The New York Times*, July 16, 1967, p. 19.

NOTES TO CHAPTER 3

1 V. P. Tugarinov, "Kommunizm i lichnost'," *Voprosy filosofii*, 1962, 6, p. 23.

2 L. V. Nikolaeva, *Lichnost' v protsesse istoricheskogo razvitiia*, Moskva: Izdatel'stvo Moskovskogo Universiteta, 1963, p. 3.

3 F. Engels, *Marx-Engels Werke*, Berlin: Dietz Verlag, vol. 20, p. 444; L. M. Mitrokhin, "Problema cheloveka v marksistskom osveshchenii," *Voprosy filosofii*, 1963, 8, p. 16.

4 Karl Marx and F. Engels, "Deutsche Ideologie," *MEGA*, vol. 5, p. 11.

5 Tugarinov, art. cit., p. 16.

6 A. S. Shishkin, *Osnovy marksistskoi etiki*, Moskva: Izdatel'stvo IMO, 1961, p. 176.

7 M. B. Mitin, "Man as Object of Philosophical Investigations," *Philosophy, Science and Man: The Soviet Delegation Reports for the XIII World Congress of Philosophy*, Moscow: Academy of Sciences of the USSR, 1963, p. 49.

8 Tugarinov, *art. cit.*, p. 14.

9 Shishkin, *op. cit.*, p. 324.

10 *Filosofskie nauki*, 1966, 6, p. 123; *Voprosy filosofii*, 1966, 9, p. 129.

11 A. F. Shishkin, "Chelovek kak vysshaia tsennost'," *Voprosy filosofii*, 1965, 1, pp. 3–15.

12 Adam Schaff, *Marksizm a jednostka ludzka*, Warszawa: Panstowe Wydawnictwo Naukowe, 1965.

13 *Socialist Humanism*, ed. Erich Fromm, New York: Doubleday & Co., Inc., 1965, p. 135.

14 *Praxis*, 1965, 2/3, pp. 187–188.

15 *Ibid.*, p. 188.

16 *Ibid.*, p. 197.

17 Karel Kosík, "Man and Philosophy," *Socialist Humanism*, pp. 148–156; *Marx and the Western World*, ed. N. Lobkowicz, Notre Dame: Notre Dame University Press, 1967, pp. 189–190.

NOTES TO CHAPTER 4

1   V. P. Tugarinov, *Lichnost' i obshchestvo,* Moskva: "Mysl',"
    1965, pp. 187–188.

2   *Philosophy, Science and Man,* Moscow: Academy of Sciences of
    the USSR, 1963, p. 71.

3   A. P. Chermenina, "Ponomanie svobody v marksistsko-leninskoi
    etike," *Filosofskie nauki,* 1964, 6, pp. 111–118.

4   *Socialist Humanism,* ed. Erich Fromm, New York: Doubleday &
    Co., Inc., 1965, p. 252.

5   *The New York Times,* August 11, 1967, p. 14.

6   *Philosophy, Science and Man,* p. 103.

7   *Voprosy filosofii,* 1963, 1, p. 23.

8   *Socialist Humanism,* p. 283.

9   *New Hungarian Quarterly,* 15 (Autumn, 1964); see also Miklos
    Almasi, "Alienation and Socialism," *Marxism and Alienation,* ed.
    H. Aptheker, New York: Humanities Press, 1965, pp. 125–142.

10 *Magyar Filozofiai Szemle,* 1966, 4.

11 *Marx and the Western World,* ed. N. Lobkowicz, Notre Dame:
    Notre Dame University Press, 1967, p. 142.

12 Adam Schaff, *A Philosophy of Man,* New York: Monthly Review
    Press, 1963, pp. 17–18. (Copyright © 1963 by Adam Schaff, re-
    printed by permission of Monthly Review Press.)

13 See my article "Heidegger and the Marxists," *Studies in Soviet
    Thought,* V (1965), pp. 289–298.

NOTES TO CHAPTER 5

1 See, for example, M. G. Zhuravkov, "XXII S'ezd KPSS i nekotorye voprosy etiki," *Voprosy filosofii*, 1962, 2, pp. 3–14; and L. F.
Il'ichev's speech of 18 June 1963, "Current Trends of the Party's
Ideological Work," *Pravda*, 19 June 1963, pp. 1–6. (English translation, *Current Digest of the Soviet Press*, 3, July 1963, pp. 5–11.)
2 A. F. Shishkin, *Osnovy marksistskoi etiki*, Moskva: Izdatel'stvo
IMO, 1961, p. 14; S. Utkin, *Ocherki po marksistsko-leninskoi etiki*,
Moskva: Sotsekgiz, 1962, p. 9.
3 A. G. Kharchev, "Moral' kak predmet sotsiologicheskogo issle-
dovaniia," *Voprosy filosofii*, 1965, 1, pp. 45–55; Shishkin, *op. cit.*
p. 48.
4 A. I. Goriacheva, "O vzaimootnoshenii ideologii i obshchestvennoi psikhologii," *Voprosy filosofii*, 1963, 11, pp. 57–65; V. N. Kol-
banovskii, "Nekotorye aktual'nye problemy obshchestvennoi
psikhologii," *Voprosy filosofii*, 1963, 12, pp. 21–23; Shishkin, *op.
cit.*, Chapter 13.
5 Il'ichev, *op. cit.*, English version, p. 10. Criticism of bourgeois
ethical theories also forms part of the basic courses in ethics. See
Programma kursa "Osnovy marksistsko-leninskoi etiki," Moskva:
Gospolitizdat, 1962.
6 The "Moral Code of the Builder of Communism" reads as follows: "The party holds that *the moral code of the builder of communism* should comprise the following principles:
     devotion to the communist cause; love of the socialist mother-
land and of the other socialist countries;
     conscientious labor for the good of society—he who does not
work, neither shall he eat;
     concern on the part of everyone for the preservation and growth
of public wealth;
     a high sense of public duty; intolerance of actions harmful to
the public interest;
     collectivism and comradely mutual assistance; one for all and all
for one;
     human relations and mutual respect between individuals—man is
to man a friend, comrade and brother;
     honesty and truthfulness, moral purity, modesty, and unpre-

tentiousness in social and private life;

   mutual respect in the family, and concern for the upbringing of children;

   an uncompromising attitude to injustice, parasitism, dishonesty, careerism and money-grubbing;

   friendship and brotherhood among all peoples of the USSR; intolerance of national and racial hatred;

   an uncompromising attitude to the enemies of communism, peace and the freedom of nations;

   fraternal solidarity with the working people of all countries, and with all peoples." (*The Road to Communism: Documents of the 22nd Congress of the CPSU*, Moscow, 1961, pp. 566–567.)

7   *Ibid.*, p. 566.

8   Morality and law are in some instances very closely related in the Soviet Union. Though negligence and tardiness are not now legally crimes, they are actions subject to the informal jurisdiction of comrades' courts.

9   See, for instance, Jaroslav Engst, *Některé problémy vědecké ethiky*, Praha: Statni Nakladatelstvi Politicke Literatury, 1957, which was translated into Russian and published in the USSR in 1960. N. Lobkowicz in his *Marxismus-Leninismus in der ČSR*, Dordrecht-Holland: D. Reidel Publishing Co., 1961, also mentions two other "reactionary and primitive" works in ethics which he considers of little value (p. 159). A Soviet review of Irina Popelova's *Etika*, Praha, 1962, cites it chiefly for its propaganda value (*Voprosy filosofii*, 1964, 8, pp. 180–181).

10   K. Gulian is the only Rumanian moral philosopher of any note and his work, some of which has been translated into Russian, is indistinguishable from the Soviet writings.

11   Hans Boeck's *Zur Marksistischen Etik und Sozialistischen Moral*, Berlin: Akademie-Verlag, 1959, was translated into Russian and published in the USSR in 1962. But it added nothing to the already existing Soviet ethical literature.

12   Adam Schaff, *A Philosophy of Man*, New York: Monthly Review Press, 1963, p. 83.

13   Milovan Djilas, *The New Class*, New York: Praeger, 1964, pp. 151–152.

14   *Inquiry*, 6 (1963), 1, pp. 18–34.

NOTES TO CHAPTER 6

1   "Materialist Dialectics is a Logic of Modern Scientific Development," *Philosophy, Science and Man,* Moscow: Academy of Sciences of the USSR, 1963, p. 98.

2   "Theory, Experimentation, Practice," *The Soviet Review,* June 1962, pp. 18–19.

3   "Aktual'nye problemy dialectiki," *Voprosy filosofii,* 1965, 10, pp. 130–164.

4   See, for example, V. S. Tiukhin, "'Kletochka' otrazheniia i otrazhenie kak svoistvo vsei materii," *Voprosy filosofii,* 1964, 2, pp. 25–34.

5   For a survey of the pertinent Soviet literature on this question, see K. G. Ballestrem, *Studies in Soviet Thought,* V (1965), pp. 139–172.

Bibliography

There are many secondary sources which trace the development of Marxist-Leninist doctrine in the Soviet Union up through the Stalinist period and somewhat beyond. The following emphasize the philosophical aspects of Marxism-Leninism: J. M. Bochenski, *Soviet Russian Dialectical Materialism (Diamat)*, trans. from the German by N. Sollohub and T. J. Blakeley, Dordrecht-Holland: D. Reidel Publishing Co., 1963; Gustav Wetter, *Dialectical Materialism: A Historical and Systematic Survey of Philosophy in the Soviet Union*, trans. from the German by Peter Heath, London: Routledge and Kegan Paul, 1958; New York: Praeger, 1959; and Richard T. De George, *Patterns of Soviet Thought: The Origins and Development of Dialectical and Historical Materialism*, Ann Arbor: The University of Michigan Press, 1966. Bertram D. Wolfe, *Marxism: 100 Years in the Life of a Doctrine*, New York: Dell Publishing Co., 1965, covers other aspects of Marxist theory in the history of its development.

For a discussion of some new developments in Soviet sociology, philosophy, cybernetics, and economics, see *Science and Ideology in Soviet Society*, ed. George Fischer, New York: Atherton Press, 1967. *Marxist Ideology in the Contemporary World: Its Appeals and Paradoxes*, ed. Milorad M. Drachkovitch, New York: Praeger, 1966; *Marxism in the Modern World*, ed. Milorad M. Drachkovitch, Stanford: Stanford University Press, 1965; and *Marx and the Western World*, ed. N. Lobkowicz, Notre Dame: Notre Dame University Press, 1967, all contain excellent surveys or analyses of the development of Marxist theories.

Marx's Concept of Man, ed. Erich Fromm, New York: Ungar, 1961, collects and introduces the basic texts of Marx on man. Adam Schaff, *A Philosophy of Man*, New York: Monthly Review Press, 1963, is one of the fullest attempts by an East European Marxist to discuss the Marxist view of man. Individual articles on man, humanism, freedom, alienation, and practice are collected in *Socialist Humanism: An International Symposium*, ed. Erich Fromm, New York: Doubleday, 1965. *Marxism and Alienation*, ed. Herbert Aptheker, New York: Humanities Press, 1965, contains a number of articles dealing with the topic of alienation, and *Existentialism versus Marxism*, ed. George Novack, New York: Dell Publishing Co., 1966, presents and relates some important statements by spokesmen for both sides.

Details of the growing body of literature on Soviet ethics are contained in my bibliography on the topic in *Studies in Soviet Thought*, III (1963), pp. 83–103, as well as in my article "Soviet Ethics and Soviet Society," *ibid.*, IV (1964), pp. 206–217. George Kline, " 'Socialist Legality' and Communist Ethics," *Natural Law Forum*, VIII (1963), pp. 21–34, relates Soviet law and ethics. Mihailo Marković, "Marxist Humanism and Ethics," *Inquiry*, VI (1963), pp. 18–34, is a statement of a Marxist position in a Western idiom.

The Soviet position on several aspects of dialectics and modern science is contained in English in several papers in *Philosophy, Science and Man: The Soviet Delegation Reports for the XIII World Congress of Philosophy*, Moscow: Academy of Sciences of the USSR, 1963. For Western discussions see Siegfried Müller-Markus, *Einstein und die Sowjetphilosophie*, 2 vols., Dordrecht-Holland: D. Reidel Publishing Co., 1960–1963; and his articles "Einstein and Soviet Philosophy," *Studies in Soviet Thought*, I (1961), pp. 78–87, and "Soviet Philosophy in Crisis," *Cross Currents*, XIV (1964), pp. 35–61. See also Loren Graham, "Quantum Mechanics and Dialectical Materialism," *Slavic Review*, XXV (1966), pp. 381–410, as well as the discussion which follows it in the same issue.

The topic of ideology has been much discussed. Some more recent statements include: J. M. Bochenski, "Toward a Systematic Logic of Communist Ideology," *Studies in Soviet Thought*, IV (1964), pp. 185–205; George Kline, "Philosophy, Ideology and Policy in the Soviet Union," *The Review of Politics*, XXVI (1964), pp. 174–190. Z. Brzezinski, *Ideology and Power in Soviet Politics*, New York: Praeger, 1962, remains an important statement, as does George Lichtheim, "The Concept of Ideology," *History and Theory*, IV (1965), pp. 164–195. Z. Brzezinski, *The Soviet Bloc: Unity and Conflict*, rev. ed., New York: Praeger, 1961, gives a very good summary of the political development of Eastern Europe since 1945.

The Institute of East European Studies, Fribourg, Switzerland, has published a number of studies of East European philosophy in its Sovietica series (Dordrecht-Holland: D. Reidel Publishing Co.), including: Z. Jordan, *Philosophy and Ideology: The Development of Philosophy and Marxism-Leninism in Poland since the Second World War*, 1963; Ervin Laszlo, *The Communist Ideology in Hungary*, 1966; N. Lobkowicz, *Marxismus-Leninismus in der ČSR, 1962;* A. Vrtacic, *Einführung in den jugoslawischen Marxismus-Leninismus*, 1963. The Institute also publishes a journal, *Studies in Soviet Thought* (vol. I– , 1961–), which carries articles devoted primarily to the study of contemporary Soviet and East European philosophy. A number of these articles have been collected in a volume, *Philosophy in the Soviet Union: A Survey of the Mid-Sixties*, ed. Ervin Laszlo, Dordrecht-Holland: D. Reidel Publishing Co., 1967.

There are a number of bibliographical guides to the enormous literature about Marxism. The most recent and complete coverage of works in English, German, and French is found in John Lachs, *Marxist Philosophy: A Bibliographical Guide*, Chapel Hill: The University of North Carolina Press, 1967. Also useful are *Doctoral Research on Russia and the Soviet Union*, ed. Jesse J. Dossick, New York: New York University Press, 1960; *Books on Communism*, ed. W. Kolarz, New York: Oxford University Press, 1964; *Bibliographie marxiste internationale*, Paris: Centre d'Études et de Recherches Marxistes, 1964– . *Bibliographie der sowjetischen Philosophie* (I– , 1959–) lists Soviet books and articles which have appeared since 1947.

A limited number of Soviet and East European works and articles have appeared in English translation. The Soviet Union publishes some works in English under the imprint of Progress Publishers, and these books are available through authorized outlets in the United States. *The Soviet Review: A Journal of Translations*, New York: International Arts and Sciences Press, 1960– , often carries translations of articles from Soviet philosophical journals; *Soviet Studies in Philosophy: A Journal of Translations*, New York: International Arts and Sciences Press, 1962– , is a quarterly devoted exclusively to such translations. The *New Hungarian Quarterly*, Budapest: Kultura, 1960– , often carries articles of philosophical interest. *Praxis: A Philosophical Journal*, Zagreb: Croatian Philosophical Society, 1965– , has an international edition which appears quarterly; it is published in English, French, and German. *Studia Filozoficzne*, Warsaw: Instytut Filozofii i Socjologii, Polska Akademia Nauk, 1957– , periodically publishes an international multi-lingual volume of selected articles, and Studia Philosophica Academiae Scientiarum Hungaricae is a series (1961–) in which one or more volumes per year of selected articles or book length manuscripts are published in English, French, German, or Russian. A few anthologies of writings by East Europeans have appeared, including *The Modern Polish Mind*, ed. Maria Kuncewicz, New York: Grosset & Dunlap, 1963. Gajo Petrović, *Marx in Mid-Twentieth Century*, New York: Doubleday & Co., 1967, contains a series of articles by one of the leading Yugoslav new Marxists.

Index